LETTERING DESIGN

Lettering

FORM & SKILL IN THE

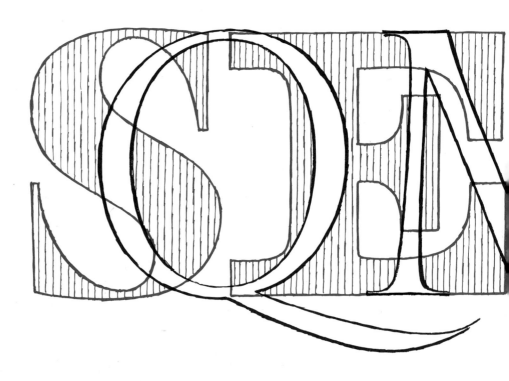

MICHAEL HARVEY

Design

DESIGN & USE OF LETTERS

FOREWORD BY JOHN RYDER

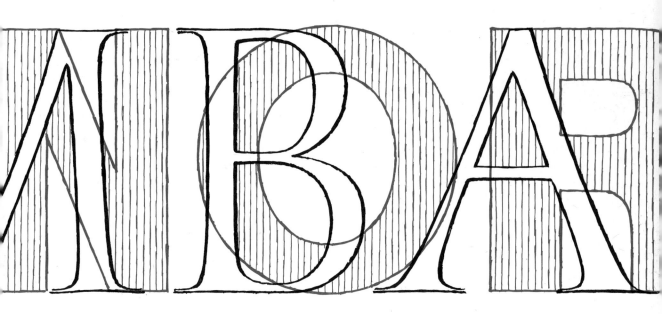

THE BODLEY HEAD
LONDON · SYDNEY · TORONTO

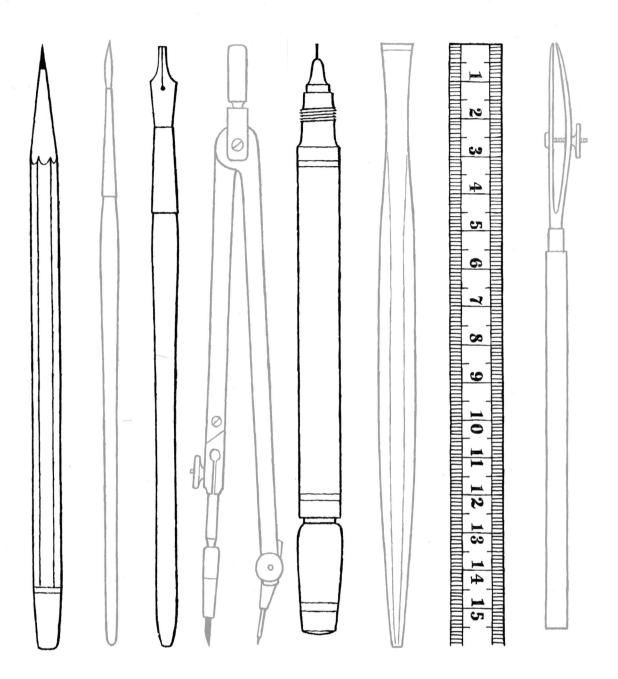

Text and drawings
© Michael Harvey 1975
ISBN 0 370 10377 7
Printed and bound in Great Britain for
The Bodley Head Ltd
9 Bow Street London WC2E 7AL
by William Clowes & Sons Ltd, Beccles
Set in Monotype Dante
First published 1975

CONTENTS

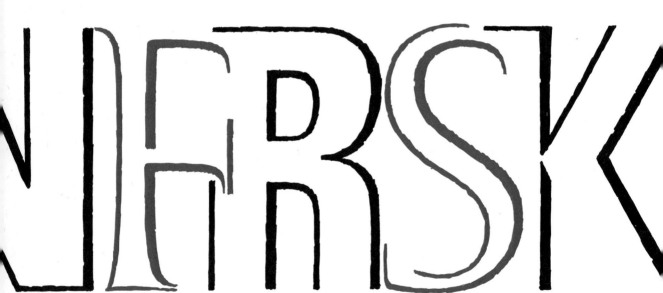

To begin with all you need to know about the letters of the roman alphabet are their basic shapes and the sounds they represent in your own language and the meaning and sounds of the words into which they are commonly combined. Recognition of word-shape eventually takes the place of reading letters and to some extent, especially in reading quickly, eliminates sound. On this slender thread of literacy an enjoyable study of lettering design can begin.

Armed with a superficial knowledge of letters an understanding of the way in which they work for us or against us, for legibility or for confusion, becomes desirable and can be reached through Harvey's book which precisely informs and equips you with a basis for criticism of a constructive kind – more, it actually draws you into what Ben Shahn so aptly described as 'the love and joy about letters'.

The discreet formal charm of roman letters, which is as much a part of our acquired culture as is the façade of a Greek temple, has remained with us virtually unchanged in 2000 or more years. It has provided the one *constant* required for the teaching of new ideas in every subject, for the communication of ideas on any level of understanding. Its importance at the centre of the dissemination of culture cannot be over-estimated and a special present-day version of the alphabet is called for – a vernacular form that is based on original inscriptional letters modified by Italian lettering of the Renaissance and by more recent variations and revivals. The Harvey model alphabets give us just that.

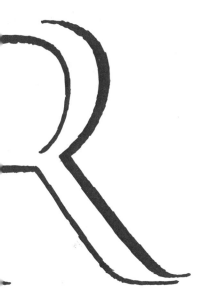

Following the discipline of letters cut in stone came the freedom of written letters which was followed by the firmer discipline of letters cast in a rigid system of metal types. Now we are back to the infinite freedom of letterforms on film where light and lenses can play all manner of tricks and deceptions. I see here in this new freedom the greatest danger to legibility unless we allow ourselves to be educated in a thorough understanding of lettering design. The temporary disappearance of this aspect of the graphic arts in technical high schools and colleges of art exaggerates the danger. To use effectively the letters of our roman alphabet it is essential to know about their origin, their geometric and optical characteristics and the practical skills of their construction. Harvey is remarkably clear on these points, and in addition, by demonstration, underlines the need for knowledge and restraint before exuberance and verve can have lasting and valued expression. He warns against the inept imitations of art nouveau and art deco lettering, against misguided distortions and against the diabolical misuse of word, letter and line spacing. He shows such practices to be mere fashion without any hope of projection into posterity.

It is my conviction that *Lettering Design* has been much needed for many years and we are indeed fortunate in finding Michael Harvey to fulfil the need. His demonstration of making and using the roman alphabet cannot fail to enlighten every reader who is lucky enough to come across this book. J.R.

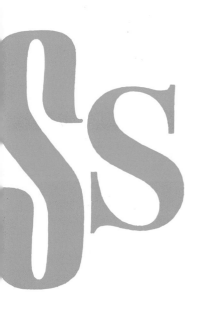

INTRODUCTION

Lettering today is a confusing variety of styles, with standards of design and practice crumbling while eccentricity flourishes. New alphabet designs, far removed from conventional forms, and revivals of styles from lettering's least distinguished periods add to the already over-crowded repertoire available to the designer. It is the first requirement of a new book on lettering that it re-establishes principles which have become blurred, and provides reliable information which will help to equip designers and users of lettering with the essential tools of the trade. At the same time it must avoid setting up a rigid and doctrinaire philosophy, even if, in the last analysis, an apparently restrictive view may sometimes emerge. Secondly, a book on lettering must recognise the needs of the contemporary world and not seek refuge in the romantic pursuit of past styles, although lettering is unique in the world of art in that yesterday's forms are used for today's purposes and history is to be seen, freshly executed, on every contemporary advertisement, sign and gravestone. As it is not possible to invent a new letter, for no one would recognise it, we re-use and adapt the forms we know, occasionally adding fresh and original variations. Therefore an awareness of historical development is essential to a real understanding of letterforms.

The third requirement is that such a book should recognise the differing needs of its readers; on the one hand the few practitioners who specialise in lettering, and on the other hand the many who use lettering in the form of type, film or transfer. These users of ready-made lettering – typographers, graphic designers, architects and others – will not want extensive instruction in the various letter-making techniques but will find their understanding and appreciation of letterforms increased by some knowledge of these skills. The specialist, given the essentials, will realise that practice alone leads to their mastery.

Fourthly, a useful book on lettering must not leave the reader at the point where he has acquired a basic understanding and appreciation of the variety of letter styles and the principles of spacing and layout. It must give general guidance on the wider aspects of design in relationship to the use of lettering in the everyday world. The intelligent and appropriate choice of lettering to suit particular needs is the hallmark of a good designer, who thereby avoids unthinking conformity to tired formulas or the equally bad, and naive, following of whatever fashion is current. The cultivation of a discriminating and informed intelligence in the reader should be the ultimate aim of any worthwhile book of this kind, and is particularly desirable when the subject is lettering, that unique and explicit combination of visual art and language.

It remains to say how this book is designed to meet the ideals I have just defined. No book of this kind can get far without making value judgements and providing examples. The model alphabets in Section 3 consist of typical letters, without mannerisms that distinguish and sometimes mar many typefaces. No typeface or ancient inscription can provide a reliable model; they were designed for other purposes and are bound to contain detail refinements out of place in a model alphabet. The choice of roman and sans serif alphabets reflects their well-established position in contemporary lettering design. The study of these alphabets is aided by the historical background in Section 2 and the detailed analysis given in Section 1 provides the reader with the necessary basic understanding of the proportions and forms of letters and the skills which shaped them. These models, like most contemporary lettering, are a product of drawing. Calligraphy no longer has any appreciable effect on the shapes of letters although a designer may incorporate calligraphic details in his drawing. Today the pencil is the universal lettering tool.

The various ways in which the shapes of letters can be modified to provide a greatly increased range of letterforms is outlined in Section 4, and opens the way to an infinite number of possible variations on the alphabets in Section 3. The designer will find his ability to distinguish the main families of letterforms improved, and can use the information given here to design his own variations.

Alphabets are only a beginning. They become 'lettering' when the letters are arranged to make words. This aspect of lettering, in which the principles of spacing and arrangement were once well-known and universally practised, has suffered from the spread of filmset and transfer letters, which, lacking the solidity of metal type, can be set extremely closely, with characters overlapping. They can, of course, also be overspaced or misaligned. While this new freedom may produce 'interesting' but illegible patterns, nevertheless it must not be forgotten that the usual purpose of lettering is to be read. In Section 5 the principles of letter, word and line spacing are illustrated, together with examples of varied and legible lettering arrangements.

The answer to any design problem, in lettering as in any other field, will be found after analysing the particular problem involved. In lettering design this analysis includes language, context, fashion and other factors. The final section of this book deals with these considerations, which every designer of lettering must take into account.

Lettering as a public art is primarily concerned with communication through language and like language itself it is subject to convention and tradition requiring widely accepted standards of form and practice. As a private art lettering may be a source of pleasure and satisfaction for those who practise its exacting skills. Choosing the right forms for a particular job (whether the letters are drawn or whether type is used) is the concern of the lettering designer. If he draws his own lettering personal control over the design will be greatly increased. Individual style in lettering is, to quote Edward Johnston, 'the natural and gradual departure from a model, and comes of practice and time'. This book provides the models, outlines the skills, deals with the principles of spacing and arrangement and aims to be of use to all concerned with lettering, whether as designers, craftsmen, teachers or simply observers and readers.

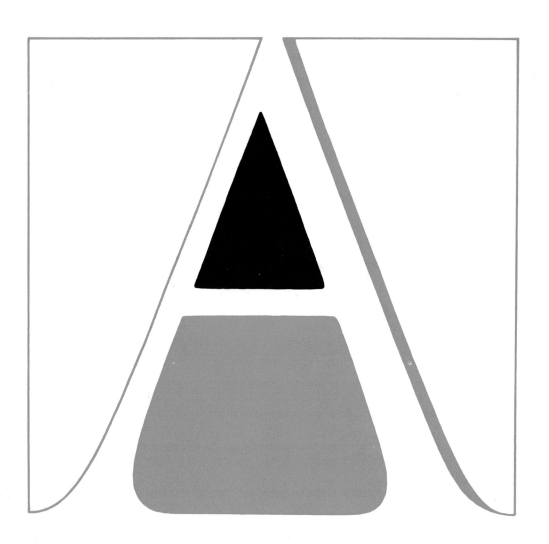

Form & Skill 1

This section contains all the information necessary for the understanding of the alphabets in Section 3. Geometric diagrams explain the basic proportions of letters and several demonstrations show the optical illusions to which letterforms are liable.

Various lettering skills such as freehand drawing, drawing with instruments and the use of brush, pen and chisel are described. Special techniques such as drawing isometric letters, letters on the curve and letters in perspective, are described for practising designers who are already familiar with letterforms.

1

2

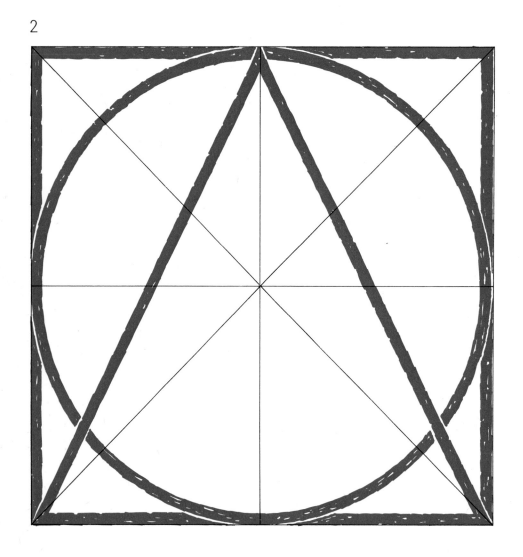

GEOMETRY/1

Basic Form

Square, circle and triangle underlie the forms of capital letters, but letters that rely merely on geometry will be visually crude. 1) These solid figures show that the square appears to be wider than the triangle and the circle, although all three figures are the same width. 2) The basic geometric units of square, circle and triangle superimposed. 3) Simple letters based on the square unit; some wide, some square and some narrow. These letters have geometric unity, but the extreme variations in width make them unsuitable as a basis for visually co-ordinated alphabets. Compare with (84).

The conclusion to be drawn from these illustrations is that the square is too wide as a basis for most letters. It should be replaced by a rectangle of narrower proportions.

3

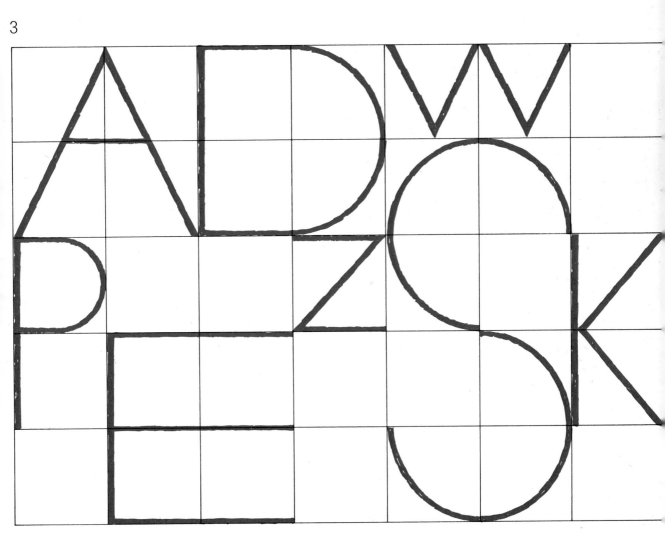

4

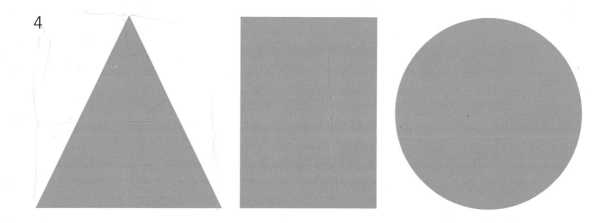

5

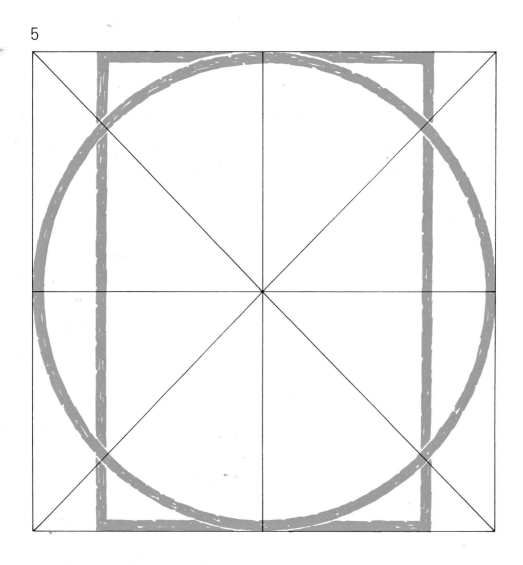

4) These solid figures show that a rectangle of approximately the same area as the circle, although narrower than the circle or the triangle, has the same visual weight as both.

5) The rectangle superimposed on the circle, each being of equal area.

6) Two rudimentary alphabets. The top alphabet has letters of varying widths, but no extreme differences. These proportions form the basis of the roman capitals in Section 3 and are also evident in (72), (73), (74), (77) and (83). The lower alphabet has letters of apparently equal width. These proportions form the basis of the sans serif capitals in Section 3 and are also evident in (81) and (85). Further refinement of these alphabets is shown below in Optics 1, 2 and 3.

6

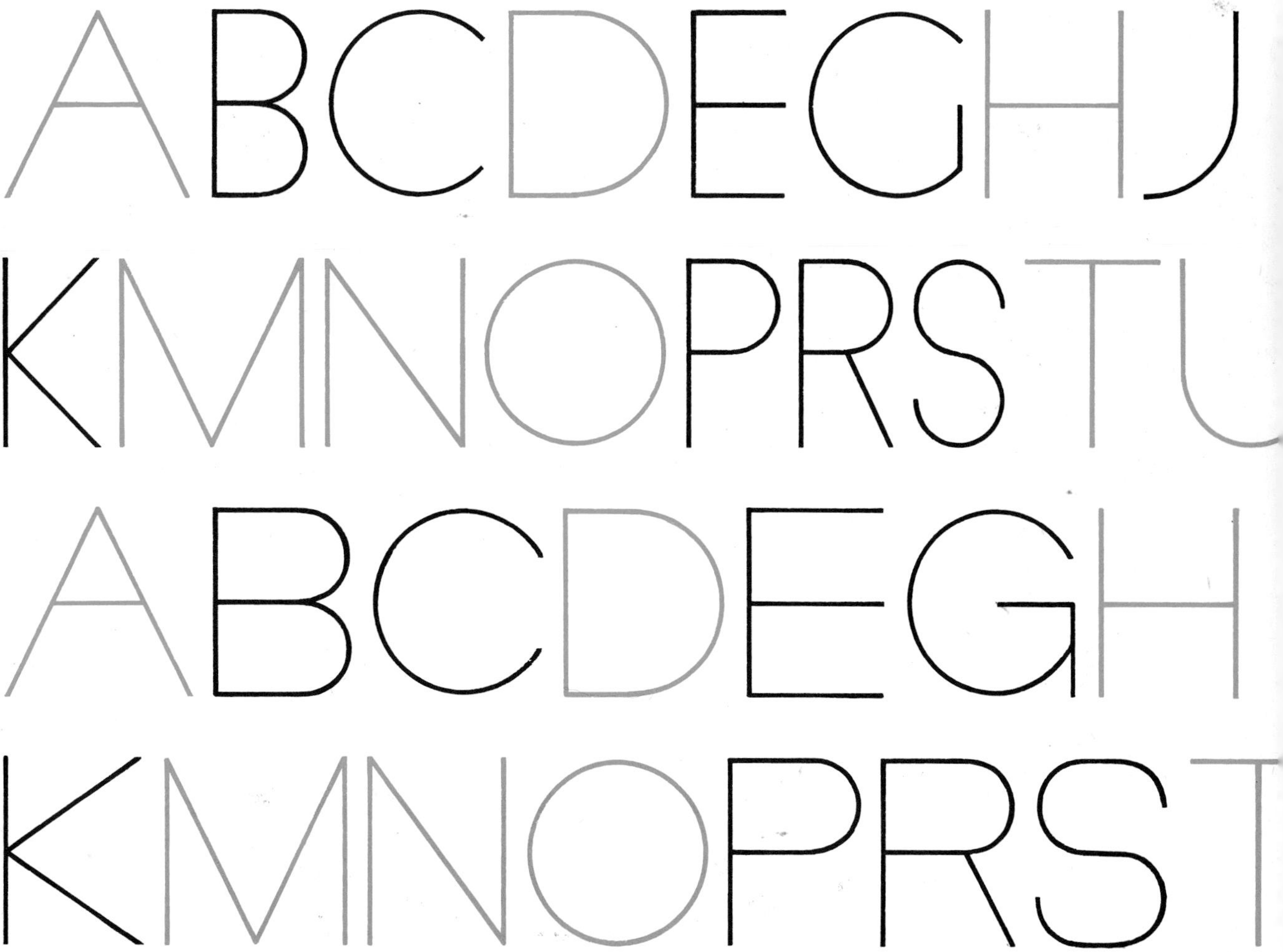

ABCDEGHJ
KMNOPRSTU
ABCDEGH
KMNOPRST

7

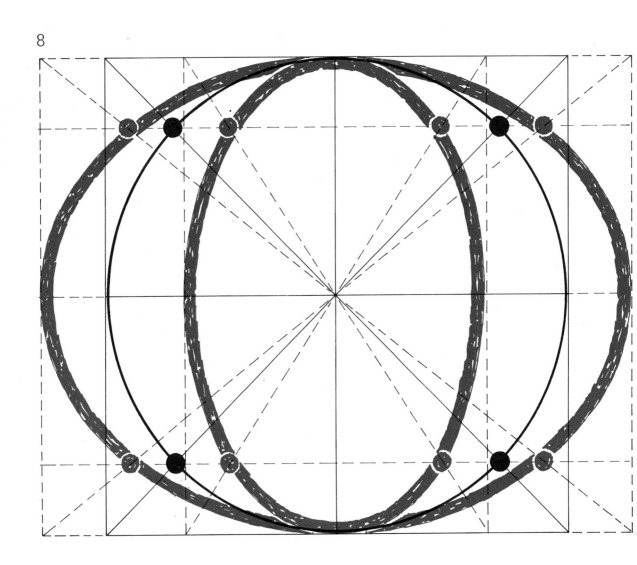

8

GEOMETRY/3

Circle and Ellipse

The system of letter structure and proportion described in Geometry 1 and 2 established a basis for the design of standard capital letters, in which curved letters are based on true circles. In alphabets of letters which are wider or narrower than standard the curved letters will be based on ellipses.

7) These solid shapes show a true circle with a condensed ellipse on the left and an extended ellipse on the right.

8) The true circle with ellipses superimposed. Notice that the four points of intersection of diagonals and curves move through a constant horizontal plane.

9) Typical letters showing elliptical curves.

These principles of construction will produce accurate ellipses. Particular letters may need slight modification to their curves to achieve a satisfactory design, and here the designer must rely on his own visual judgement.

9

BSO

BSO

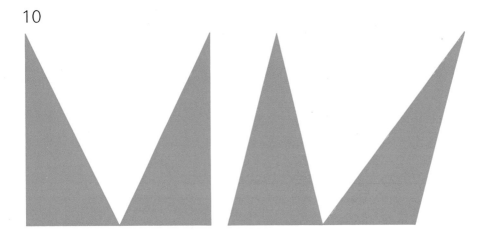

10

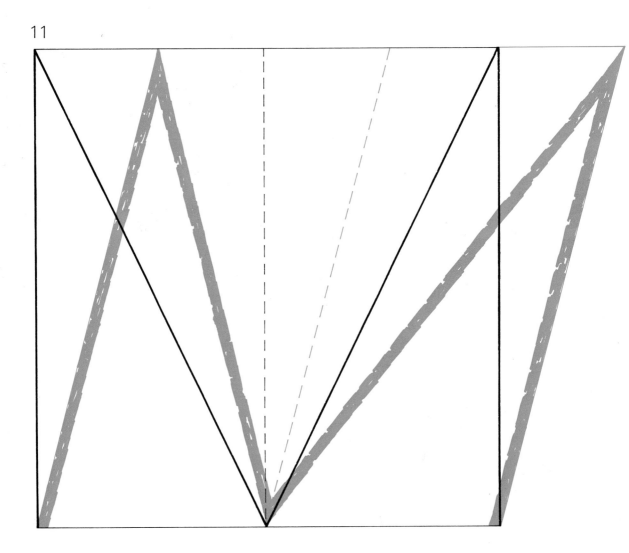

11

The structure of letters with diagonal strokes is considerably altered when the letter is inclined from the vertical.

10) These solid triangles represent the inner shapes of letter M; on the left the usual vertical form, on the right the inclined form. The equal, balanced shapes in the vertical form become unequal in the inclined version, but in both cases the areas are equal.

11) The vertical letter M with the inclined letter superimposed. The width of the letter on the base line remains the same and so does the position of the point of the central vee, but the angles which are equal in the vertical position are unequal in the inclined.

12) Typical letters in which diagonals occur, vertical and inclined. See also (78).

12

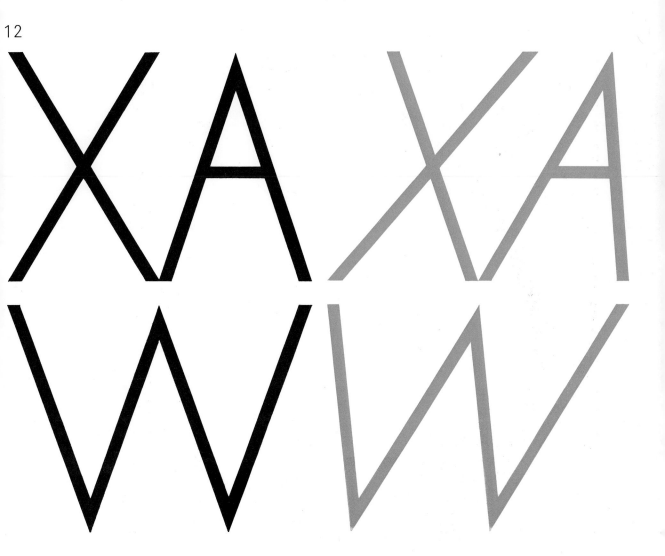

13

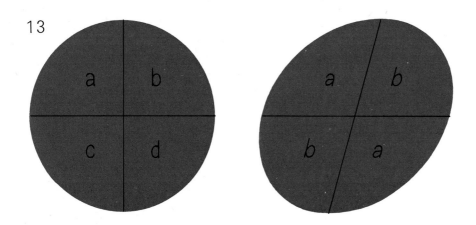

14

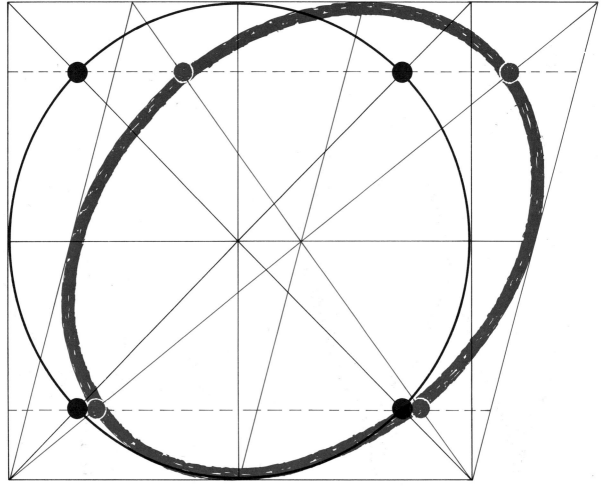

Inclined Curves

The circumference of a circular letter changes shape when the letter is inclined from the vertical.

13) These solid shapes demonstrate the differences between a circle and its inclined counterpart. The upright circle has four equal segments (a,b,c,d,), while the inclined one has two pairs of equal segments (a,a, and b,b,), diagonally opposed. All segments in both shapes are of the same area.

14) The true circle with the inclined version superimposed. This is an ellipse whose major axis is the longer diagonal of the parallelogram. The four points of intersection of diagonals and curves move through a constant horizontal plane.

15) Typical curved letters, vertical and inclined. See also (78).

These illustrations show that fundamental changes take place when a curved letter is inclined; a vertical letter that is tilted without structural change will not look satisfactory.

15

DCS

DCS

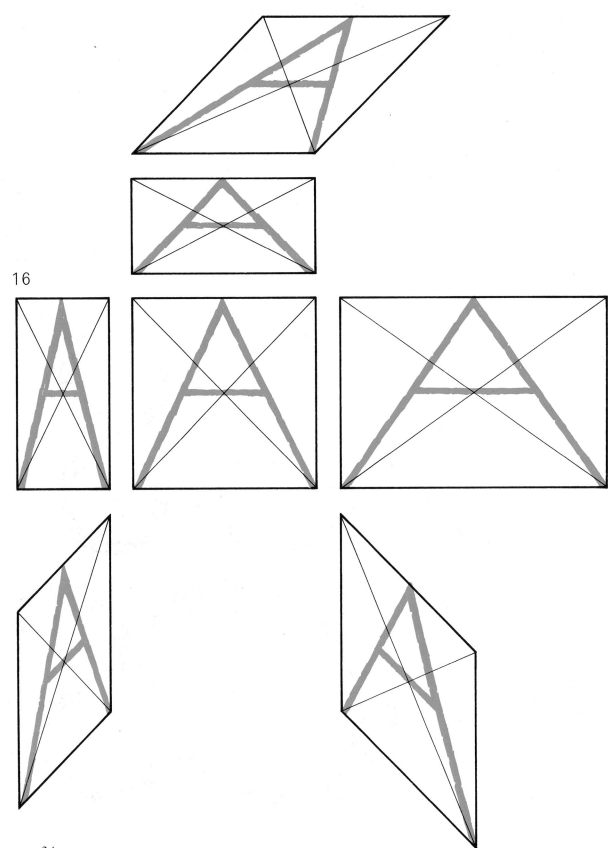

16

Condensed, Extended and Isometric Letters

Letterforms that are condensed or extended versions of the standard letters should maintain their basic structural relationships within a rectangular grid. In isometric letters this grid is a parallelogram.

16) The letter A in a square is the standard form; the rectangles and parallelograms contain condensed, extended and isometric versions. In each case the apex of the letter remains in the middle of the top line, and the cross-bar remains parallel with the top and base lines.

17) This figure in isometric projection has three planes which contain inclined letters. B inclines to the left; A and C incline to the right. See Geometry 4 and 5 for further details.

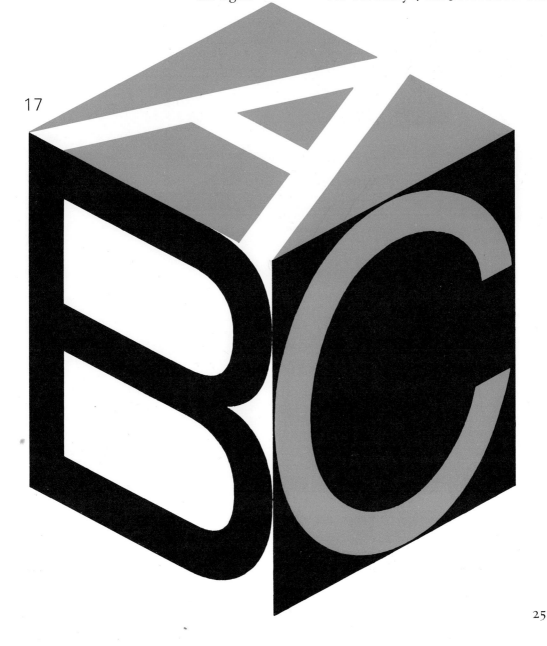

17

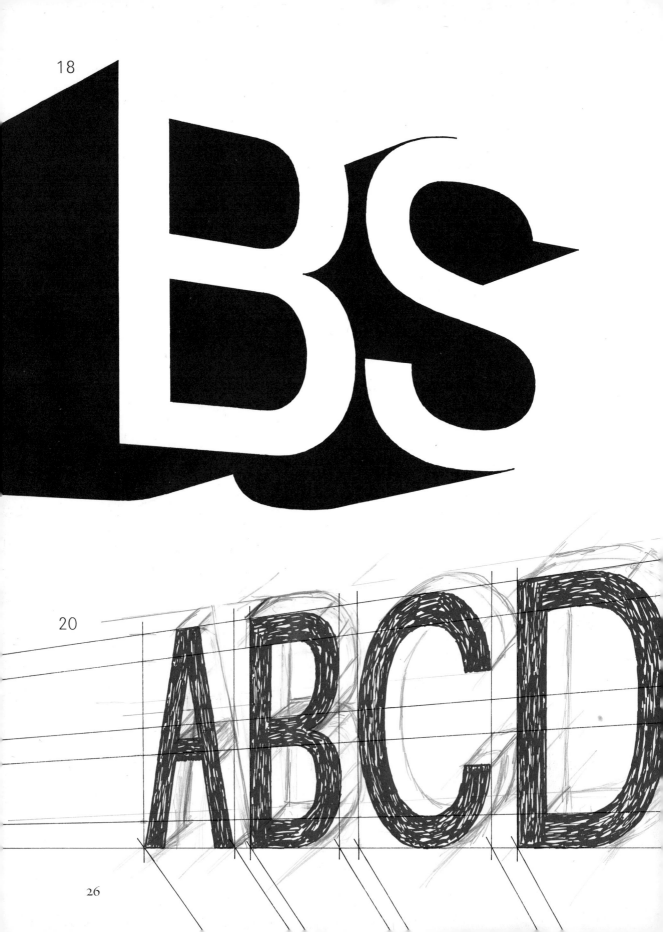

Letters in Perspective

Letters can be treated as objects in space and drawn according to the normal laws of perspective.

18) A three-dimensional effect which uses two vanishing points.

19) This plan shows an easy way to achieve accurate perspective. CB is the base line of letters marked off in letter-widths and spaces; AB is the plane on which the letters are to be seen; D is the viewing position. Lines drawn from CB to D bisect AB giving the positions of the perspective letters.

20) Letters constructed as described above. Horizontal guide-lines for letter heights are marked off on the right-hand side and continued in perspective to a vanishing point on the left. Any degree of perspective can be used but great accuracy is needed where the angle is acute.

19

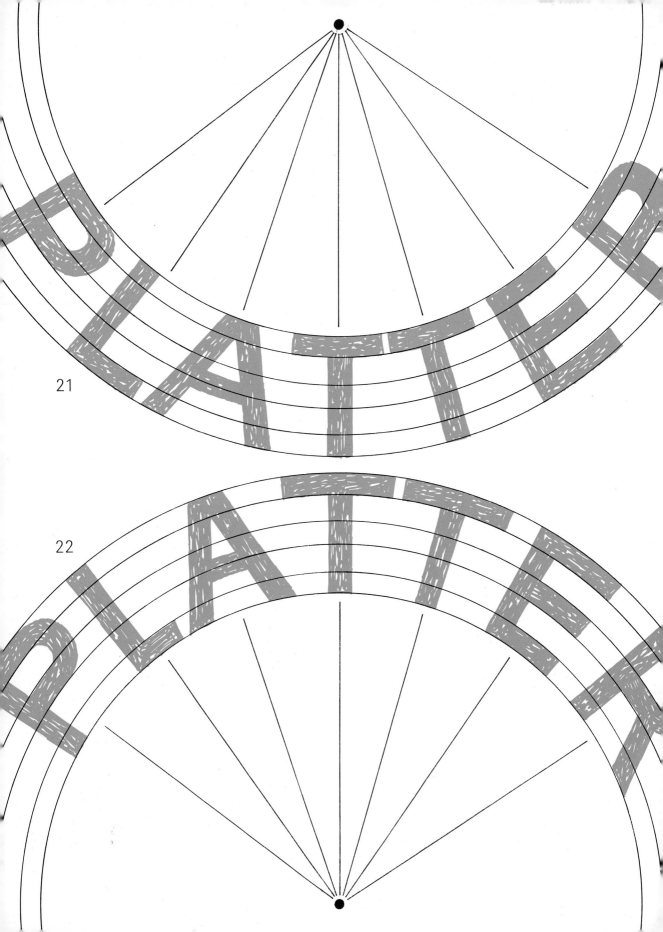

21

22

GEOMETRY/8

Letters on a Curve

Letters drawn around a curve must be modified to maintain even spacing.

21) Letters on a convex curve. The space between TT is reduced by shortening the horizontal strokes. The horizontal strokes on E are extended slightly to maintain the radial effect. A is wider than usual.

22) Letters on a concave curve. The horizontal strokes of TT are extended along the outer curve. The horizontal stroke of L is shortened to reduce the space between itself and A. A is narrower than usual.

23) Roman capitals have the advantage that their serifs emphasise and maintain the circular effect and can join where necessary.

23

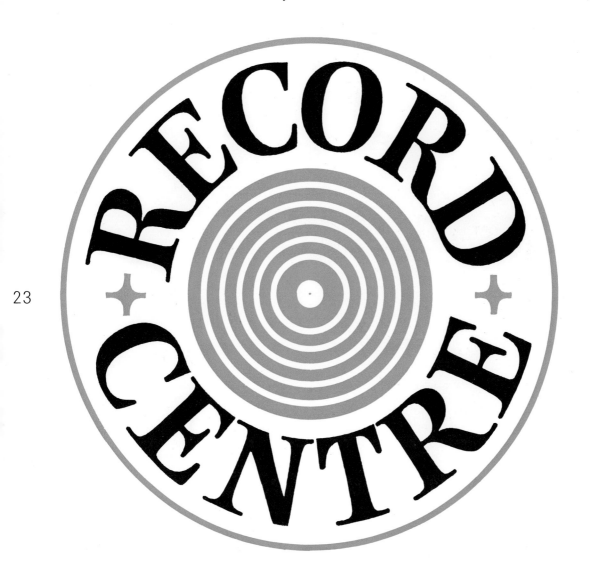

VZA
HE
ODV

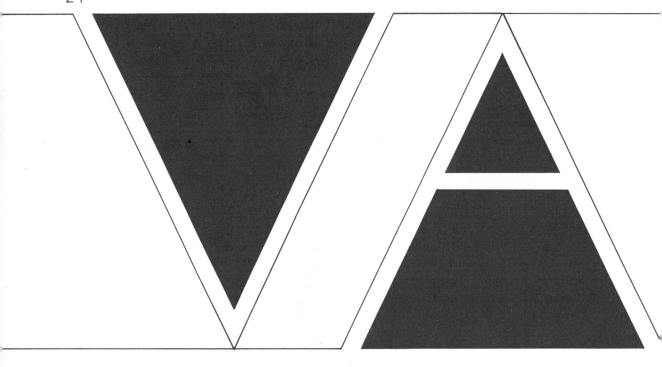

Pointed and Curved Letters

In a normal line of lettering the lack of horizontal strength in pointed and curved letters makes them appear too short. A similar illusion is apparent in the vertical alignment of letters.

24) The apexes of A and V and the curves of O appear not to align with wide horizontal forms. Here the solid inner shapes emphasise this illusion.

25) Points and curves cross into the margins to improve alignment. See also (73), (78) and (83). Lettering arrangements having several lines of the same length or ranging left or right from a common vertical should be aligned vertically in this manner, as can be seen in (158), (160), (161) and (167). It is important that these various corrections for optical illusions should not be over-done.

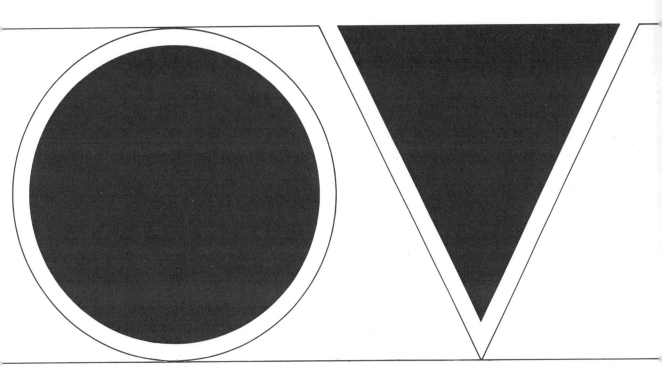

27

H R
E S
K X

28

B

26

Two-Storey Letters

The top halves of two-storey letters and figures appear too large when the letters are divided horizontally in equal proportions. 26) The horizontal divisions, which are central, appear to be lower. The top halves appear larger, and, in letters B and K, wider than the bottom halves.

27) Typical two-storey letters with the horizontal division raised to the optical centre line above the actual centre line (shown dotted). This fractional difference is vital. The letters are now optically balanced.

28) The top half of B is slightly narrower than the bottom, correcting the illusion shown in (26). Letters K, R, S, X and figures 3 and 8 need the same modification.

31

BS E
a drm

29

T
O
T
O

Weight and Thickness

In letters in which all strokes have the same weight and thickness several illusions occur.

29) Horizontal strokes, straight and curved, appear to be thicker than vertical strokes of the same width. These are shown in black. A slight reduction in the actual thickness of the horizontal strokes removes this illusion. In a circular letter the inside shape becomes an ellipse.

30) At the junctions of straight and curved strokes, and of two curved strokes, an excess of weight is apparent. These are shown in black. A progressive reduction in the radii of the outer curves as they meet the junction will cure this visual defect.

31) Capital and lowercase letters in which these modifications have been made. In the extended capital E the long horizontals have been considerably reduced in thickness to lessen their extra weight.

30

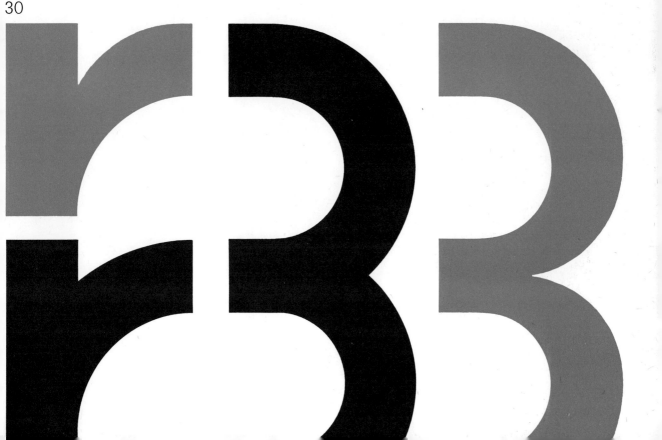

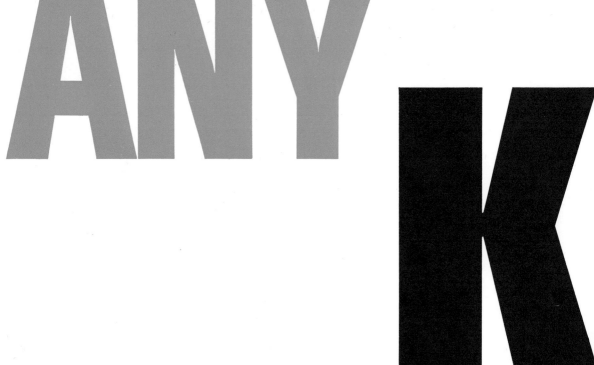

The apexes of even-weight letters become too heavy in any but the lightest forms, a problem which is accentuated in the case of condensed letters.

32) In the black letters the stroke junctions overlap completely, producing in the more acute angles an excess of weight. The spaces inside M are very unbalanced, the top space being much too large and the bottom spaces too small. In V the space is fast disappearing. In the coloured letters the strokes do not overlap completely. The junctions are wider than the stroke width, weight is more evenly distributed, and the inside shapes are better balanced. In V the inside strokes are slightly tapered and curved to bring the inside point down as far as possible.

33) Typical condensed letters using these modifications. In N the vertical strokes are thinner than the diagonal to reduce the overall weight of the letter. The junction of the diagonal strokes with the vertical in this K is very slight, and the diagonal strokes are fractionally tapered to allow the maximum amount of space inside this bold, condensed letter.

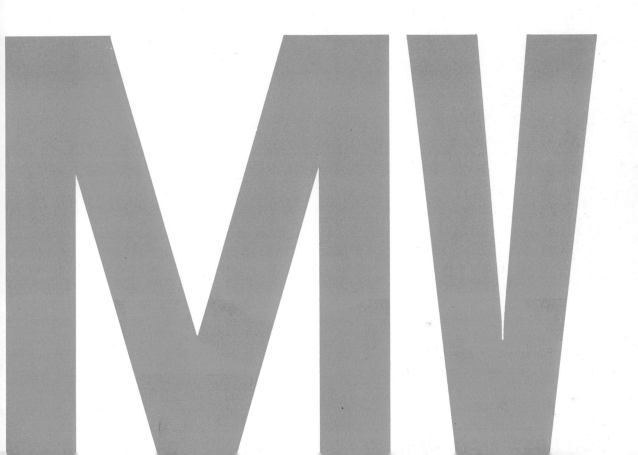

LA AV TA
TT IM LY
TY CI

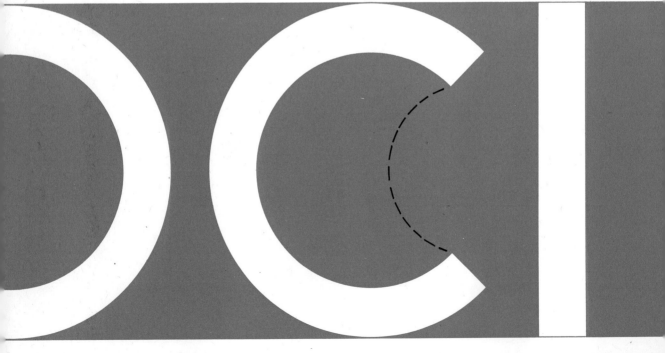

Spaces between Letters

Irregular areas are created between letters when they are spaced equidistantly, and these areas must be given some uniformity of visual weight if words are to be legible and balanced in appearance. This can best be achieved by visual judgement rather than measurement.

34) Basic letter combinations: vertical with vertical; vertical with curve; curve with curve; open curve with vertical; vertical with diagonal. These are arranged to give visually equal spacing; the markers at the foot of the page indicate the actual distances between the letters. In the open curve of C only part of the space is effective in letter spacing, as shown by the dotted line. See also (83) and (140) for even spacing of roman capitals.

35) Letter combinations with unavoidably large spaces.

36) Letter combinations with almost no space. In a word all these combinations would cause great unevenness. Although large spaces are often unavoidable, spacing out the other letters in the word will lessen the bad effect.

37) Letters which overlap slightly to reduce space; an effect that can be achieved with film, transfer and drawn letters, but not with printing type.

Examples of the unbalanced effect of equidistantly spaced letters abound, typewritten letters and car number-plates being the most obvious.

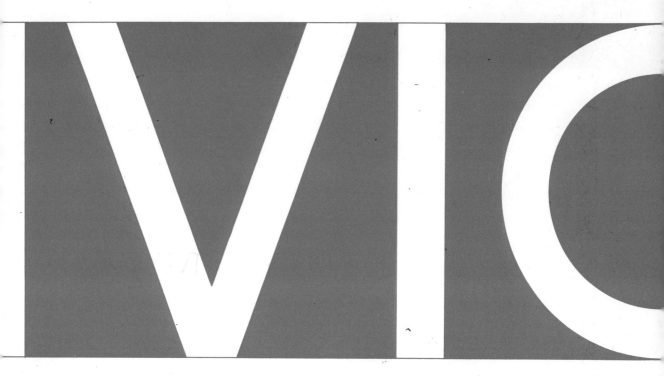

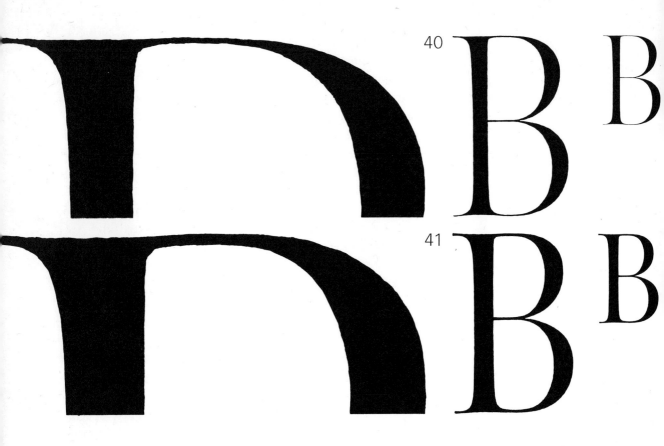

38

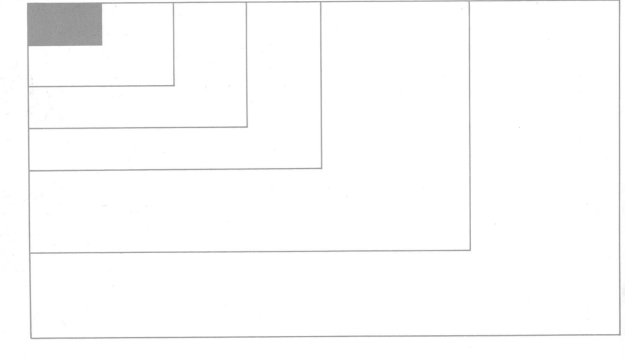

Photographic reduction can produce a serious loss of weight in letters.

38) The ratio between linear and area reduction is 1:2; when a rectangle is reduced to half its original size the area becomes a quarter of the original. This relationship between linear measurement and area is maintained whatever the change in size.

39) Letters losing weight as they are progressively reduced in size.

40) A fine letter when reduced becomes too light in appearance and its thinner strokes are almost lost.

41) A slightly bolder letter reduces more successfully.

The weight loss described here is well known to typedesigners, who draw small sizes of type bolder to compensate. For this reason small type photographically enlarged often looks heavy and clumsy.

39

B B B
B B B

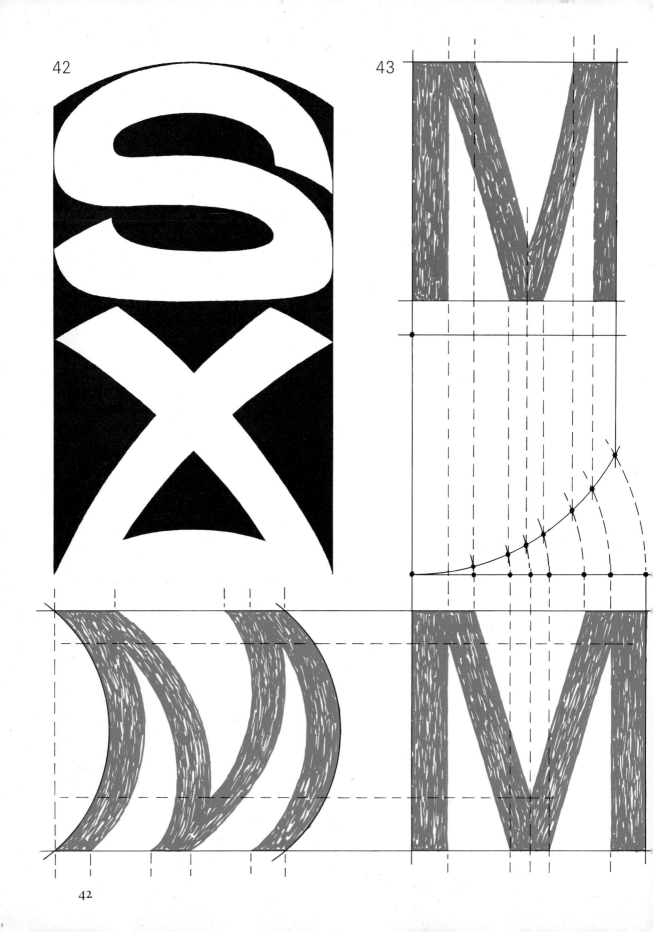

42

Letters designed to create a spatial illusion, or to be seen from a particular viewpoint.

42) Letters on an apparently curved surface.

43) The standard form of capital M is projected horizontally and vertically on to curves, producing an illusion of curved letters, and, in the vertical version, a degree of foreshortening. In both cases the letter height remains the same as in the original.

44) A common road-marking. Designed to be seen from an approaching car, the original on the road surface is distorted to give the driver the illusion that he is reading normal letters. This built-in allowance for foreshortening is also used for lettering on tall buildings, and in other situations where the angle of view is likely to be acute.

44

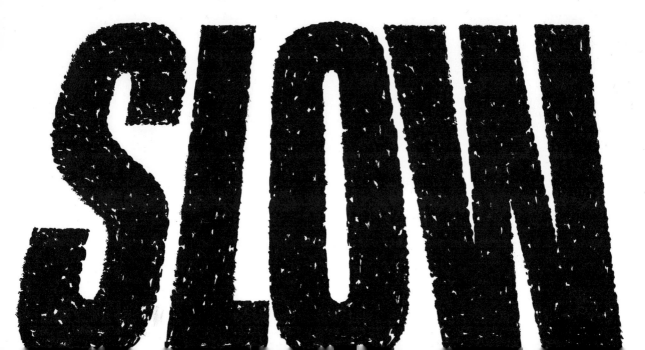

45

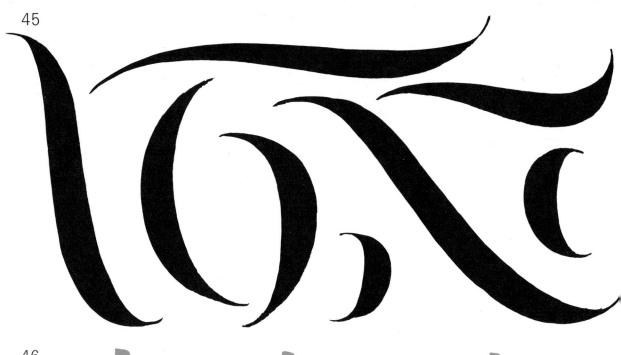

46

abcdefghij

47

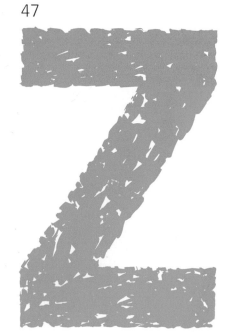

48

ZIIII

TECHNIQUE/1

The Brush

The pointed brush is a very versatile and flexible letter-making tool.

45) Characteristic brush strokes, varying in thickness according to the pressure applied.

46) Letters made from simple brush strokes.

47) Informal roughness achieved by jerky brush movements. Compare with (63), (77), (91) and (98).

48) The sequence of brush strokes in a built-up letter, in which the serifs are an integral part. This signwriter's technique, in which wrist movements control the brush, can be used with finger control for drawing quite small letters. Compare with (74).

49) An analysis of a Roman R based on the work of E. M. Catich, in which economical brush strokes produce a letter of great elegance. The initial and final strokes of the brush make the serifs an essential part of the letter. The finished version of the letter is shown in colour. Compare with (73) and (83).

The brush is best used as a tool in its own right, and not just to fill in pencilled outlines. In fact an outline gives no indication of the substance of the finished letter, which a brush can instantly provide.

See also the description of drawing technique given on pages 52 and 53.

49

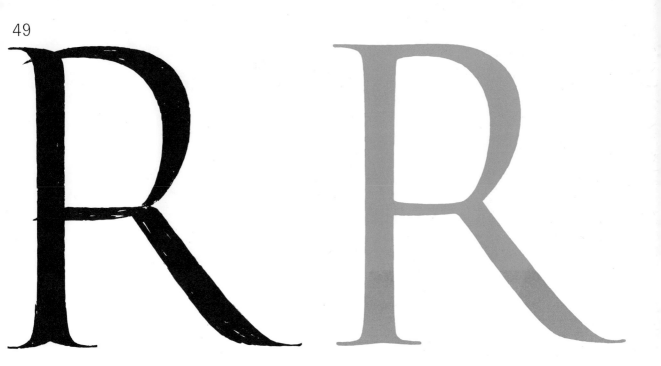

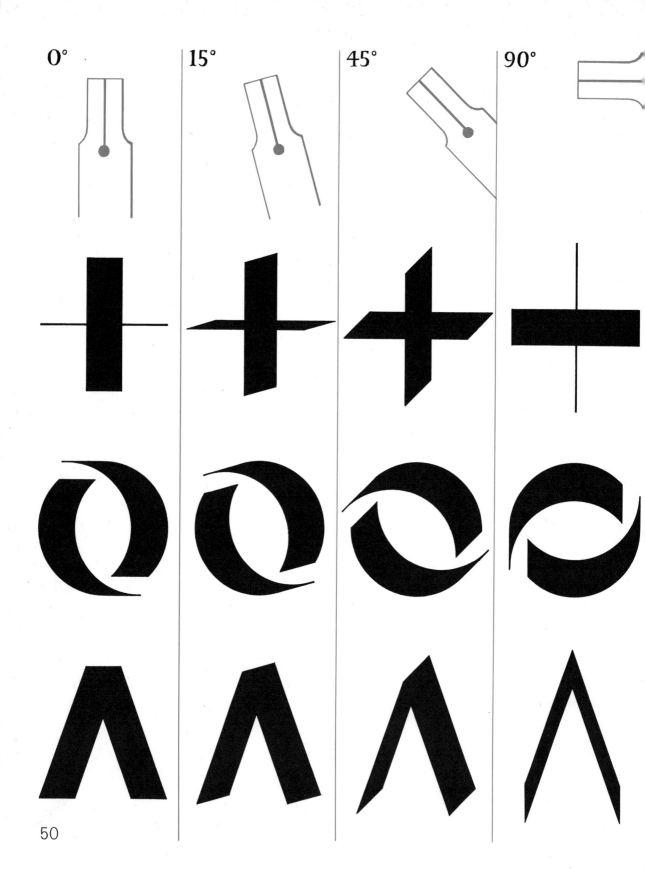

0° 15° 45° 90°

50

46

The broad-edged pen's main characteristics are contrasting thick and thin strokes.

50) A pen held without tilt produces thick verticals and thin horizontals. Curves are thinnest at the top and thickest at the sides. Diagonals are slightly thinner than verticals. A tilt of 15 degrees produces slightly thinner verticals and thicker horizontals. Curves have a pronounced 'stress'. Diagonals are slightly thinner on the left and thicker on the right. A tilt of 45 degrees extends the process. Horizontals and verticals are the same thickness. Curves have a stronger 'stress'. Diagonals are much thinner on the left and thicker on the right. A tilt of 90 degrees reverses the original effect. Horizontals are thick and verticals are thin. Curves are thickest at the top and thinnest at the sides. Diagonals are of equal thickness. This diagram demonstrates the main pen angles, but in practice these vary within a piece of writing.

51) Letters made with a pen angle of approximately 15 – 20 degrees, the angle most common in writing because it is the easiest to maintain without fatigue. The roman lowercase alphabet in Section 3 is based on these pen forms.

52) Letters made without a tilt. Compare this S with the S in (51).   See also (86), (87), (88), (89), (90) and (92).

51

Snee

52   mos

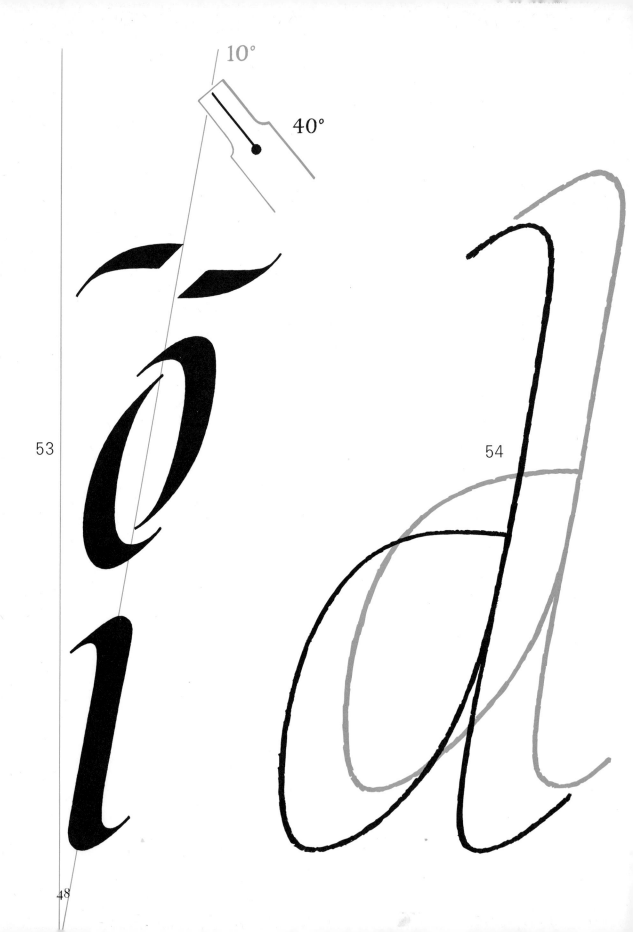

10°

40°

53

54

48

Characteristics of the broad pen structure of italic script.

53) With a letter angle of 10 degrees and a pen angle of 40 degrees horizontal and vertical strokes are nearly the same thickness and thin strokes are at 40 degrees. The thickest part of the stroke will be at the points where the pen moves through 40 degrees at the top and bottom of each letter stroke. Curved strokes are flattened; lefthand strokes are thin at the top and thick at the bottom, righthand strokes are thick at the top and thin at the bottom.

54) This outline letter, tracing the paths of the pen's left and right corners, gives a clear picture of the letter structure.

55) The inner shapes – 'counters' – of italic letters are narrow and elliptical.

56) The inner and outer shapes of italic *a*. *aa* is the letter angle (10 degrees); *bb* is the diagonal axis; *cc* is the pen angle (40 degrees) which determines the angle of the serif and the thin strokes. These structural characteristics are the basis of the italic lowercase alphabet in Section 3. See also (97) and (102).

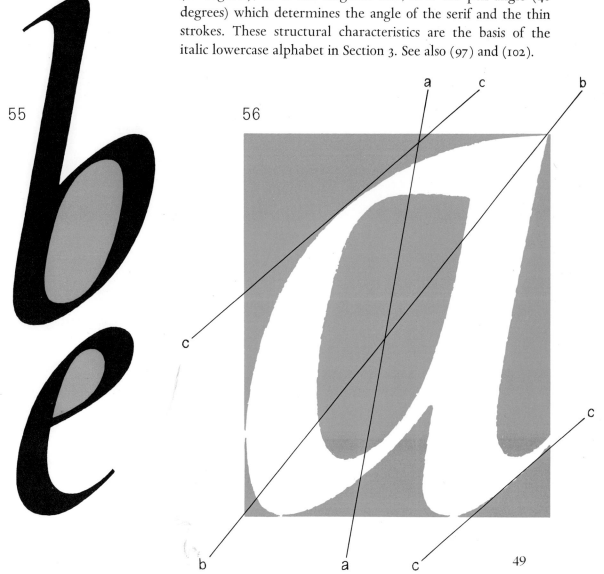

55

56

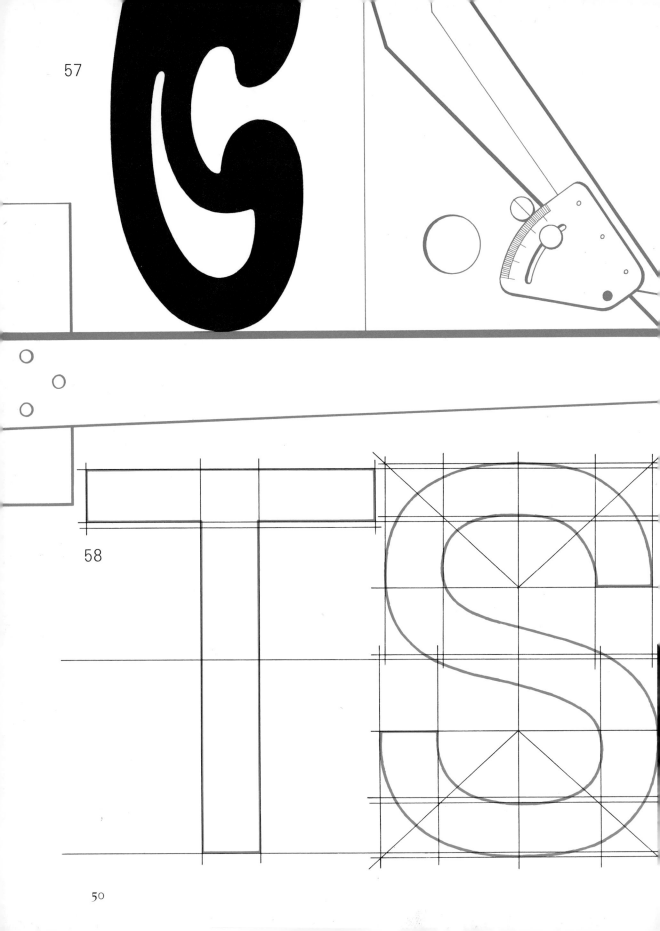

57

58

TECHNIQUE/4

Drawing with Instruments

Drawing instruments are used for drawing letters with a mechanical appearance, such as the sans serif alphabets in Section 3. See also (84), (85) and (95).

57) T-square, adjustable set square, compasses and french curves. To these may be added a clearly calibrated rule, an eraser and assorted pencils – hard pencils for guidelines, and softer ones for sketching curves. Drawings for reproduction will be done in Indian ink, using a ruling pen for outlines, a brush for filling in and white paint for re-touching.

58) The preliminary guidelines for letters TS. All the essential information is accurately drawn, and the various modifications described on pages 30–35 have been made. The curves are too complex to be drawn with compasses and have been sketched freehand before finishing with the aid of french curves.

59) The finished letters.

When drawing letters in outline it is important to ensure that the outline is part of the finished letter and not part of the background, otherwise the letter will be too heavy when filled in solid. Any errors should be corrected when the filling in is completed as it is difficult to assess the degree of error in an unfinished drawing.

59

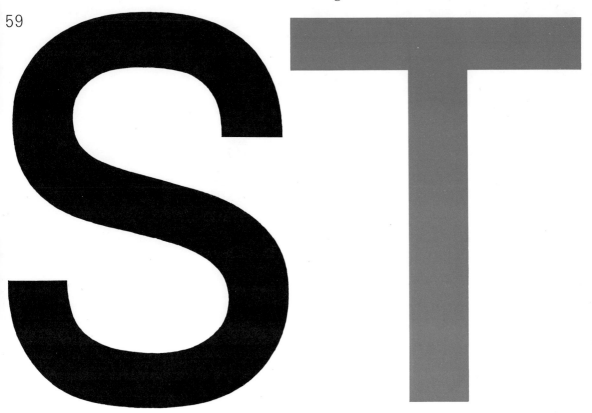

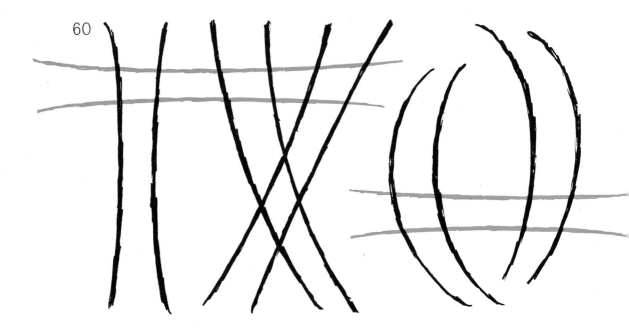

60

61 ABCDEFG

62

TECHNIQUE/5

Drawing Freehand

The roman and italic alphabets in Section 3, and most of the lettering in this book, have been drawn freehand.

60) Characteristic freehand drawing strokes. The hand should rest on the drawing surface and the fingers be allowed to guide the pencil freely.

61) Letters which exploit the hand's natural ability to draw vigorously and freely, without guidelines. See also (160) and (178) and compare with (72).

62) Two capital letters; the lefthand letter drawn freehand, the righthand one with instruments. The freehand version, although done with great care and precision, is graceful and alive, while the other is hard and lifeless.

63) The style of drawing can change the character of a letter. Here a normally smooth calligraphic initial is drawn with a rough texture. Compare with photographically enlarged type (77), (91), (98) and (100), also (47), (150), (180) and (185).

64) Letters with a free and fluid outline, illustrating the control of form, line and space that is possible with freehand drawing. See also (82) and (173).

Drawing is used to produce most contemporary lettering, whether it be printing type, transfer letters, film letters or artwork for reproduction. When we speak of designing letters we imply that this will be done by drawing.

63

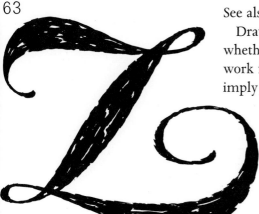

64

SMITH

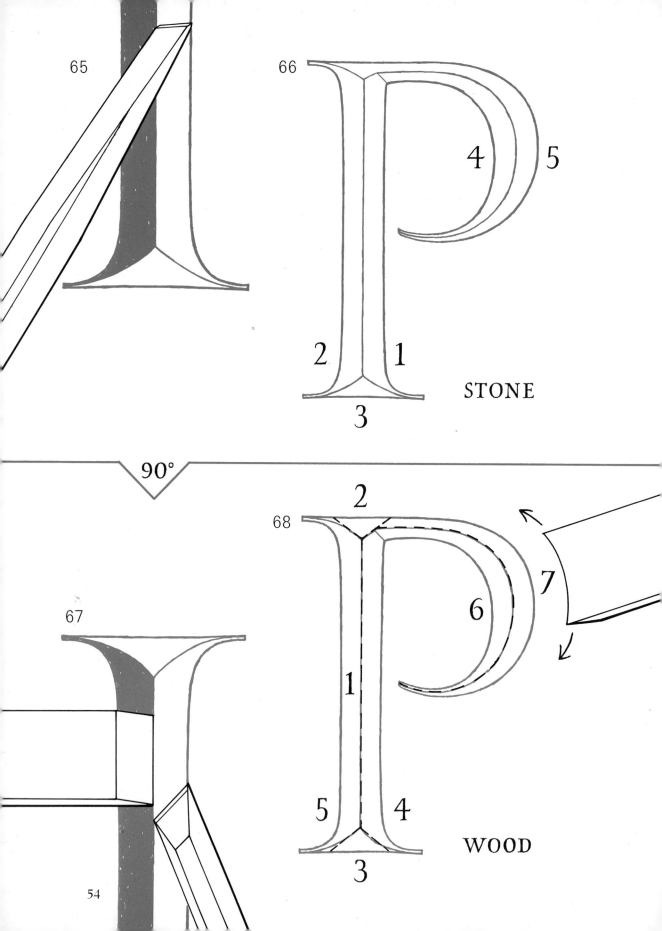

65

66

4　5

2　1

3

STONE

90°

67

68

2

6　7

1

5　4

3

WOOD

54

Letters in Stone and Wood

The inscriptional letter has a long history (see page 59) and the technique of letter cutting has remained unchanged from early times.

65) In stone a narrow chisel cuts a vee section of approximately 90 degrees. The depth of cut will vary according to the width of the stroke. The stone should be in a vertical position.

66) The sequence of cuts for a letter P.

67) In wood a wide chisel cuts vertically down into the centre of the stroke. A narrower chisel cuts out triangles of wood to form serifs and removes the waste wood to make a vee section. The wood should be in a horizontal position.

68) The sequence of cuts for a letter P; a gouge of the right curvature removes the waste wood from the outside of curved strokes.

69) A rubbing from an inscription.

70) A drawn letter which suggests the light and shadow of the inscriptional form. See also (73).

71) An inscriptional letter, unless it is painted, relies on light and shade for definition.

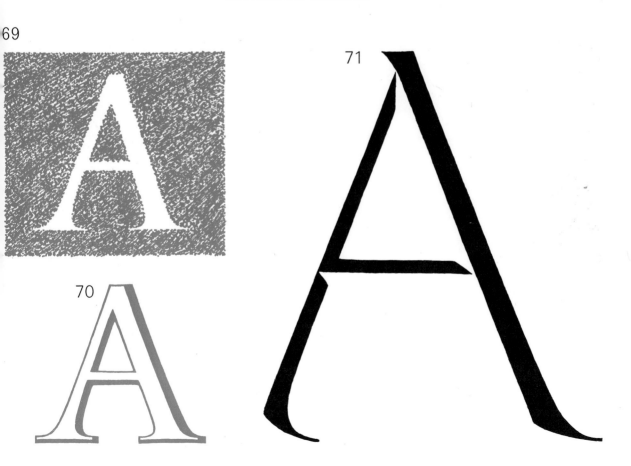

69

70

71

FURTHER READING

Catich, Edward M., *The Origin of the Serif*, The Catfish Press, 1968
Johnston, Edward, *Writing and Illuminating and Lettering*, Pitman, 1906
    Formal Penmanship, Lund Humphries, 1971
Kaech, Walter, *Rhythm and Proportion in Lettering*, Walter-Verlag, 1956
Fairbank, Alfred, *A Handwriting Manual*, Faber and Faber, 1954
Gourdie, Tom, *Handwriting for Today*, Pitman, 1971
    Puffin Book of Lettering, Penguin Books, 1961
Thomson, George L., *Better Handwriting*, Penguin Books, 1954

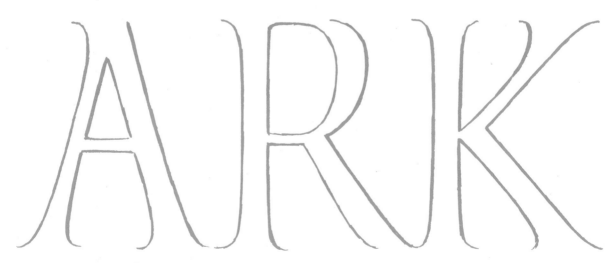

The line defines the letter —
the inside spaces and the shapes between

Historical Sources 2

To gain a real understanding of the alphabets in Section 3 it is necessary to be aware of their historical origins, and the reasons for their general acceptance today. The brief histories of capitals, lowercase and italic given in this section are necessarily simplified, but the reader is advised to follow up this introduction by studying some of the books listed on page 74. History is an endless source of forms, ideas and practice from which today's designers can draw guidance and inspiration.

CORNELIVS

CAESA

R·IMP·

VERBV

The letters that we know as capitals began as crude geometric forms with even weight strokes and no serifs. These early forms, introduced by the Phoenicians and Greeks and adopted by the Romans, were developed in the first century AD into majestic inscriptional letters of great sophistication. Painted on stone by a signwriter they were subsequently carved by a mason, the strokes finely cut in a vee section (see Technique 6).

With the decline of the Roman Empire this inscriptional letter was less used, although drawn capitals survived as initial letters in manuscript books. The late medieval capital, known as *blackletter*, was far removed from the classic roman letter. During the Renaissance in fifteenth century Italy the roman capital was used again on buildings, coins and medals, and became a model for early printing types.

72) Early inscriptional roman capitals, second century BC.

73) Classic inscriptional roman capitals from the first century AD, which combine calligraphic grace and geometric principles. See (49).

74) Manuscript initials drawn with a pen or brush. See (48).

75) Gothic capital from the fourteenth to the fifteenth century. See also (192).

76) Renaissance geometry – one of many systems for designing capital letters. This R by Francesco Torniello of Novara (after Pacioli) was published in 1517.

75

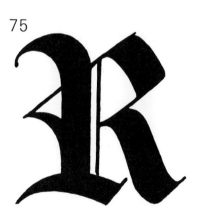

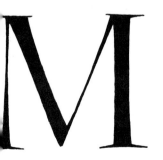

76

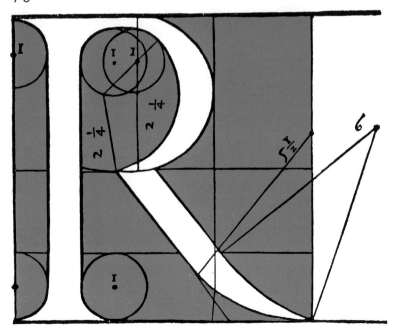

PRIN

BASKERV

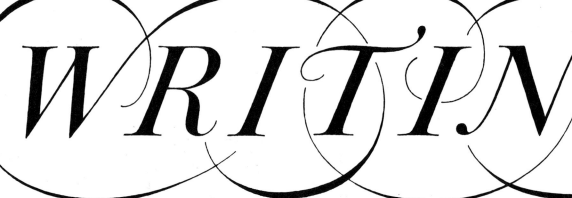

WRITIN

EE

CAPITAL LETTERS

16th Century to
19th Century

The first typefaces produced in Italy were relatively simple, but by the eighteenth century typefaces were much more refined.

In the nineteenth century, bold versions of roman typefaces were made, as well as many decorative variations. The most significant development was the sans serif typeface. Sans serif letters existed in early roman times and during the Renaissance.

77) Typical early sixteenth century type.

78) This refined mid-eighteenth century type of John Baskerville has considerable contrast between the thick and thin strokes. Baskerville was printer, calligrapher and lettercutter, and a drawn version of his carved italic capitals is shown here.

79) Nineteenth century letters, *Fatface*, see also (111) and *Ionic*, see also (108). Compare these with the E in (78).

80) Typical nineteenth century decorative letters in the *Tuscan* style. See also (126).   81) Sans serif type design, 1832.

80

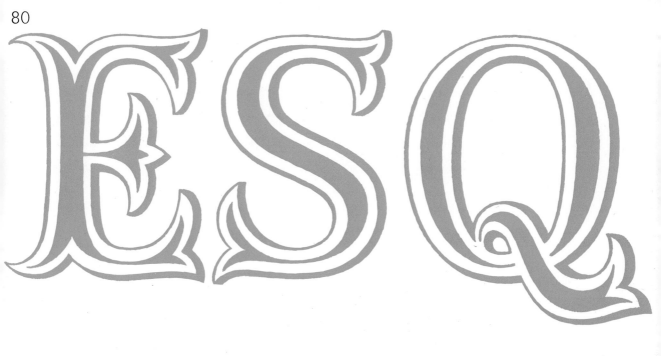

81

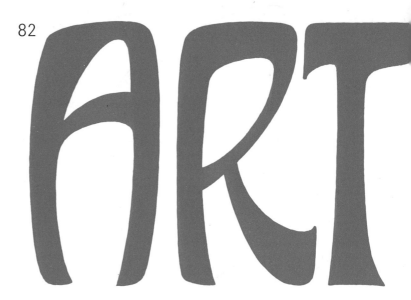

82 ART

83 MUSEU

84 AST

A reaction against the nineteenth century proliferation of lettering styles, particularly Art Nouveau, spurred an international revival of interest in classic roman letters in the early 1900's. Among the typefaces that have resulted from this revival are Eric Gill's *Perpetua*, Hermann Zapf's *Palatino* and Giovanni Mardersteig's *Dante*. In the 1920's experiments in geometric lettering led to a fashion in machine-like sans serif forms.

82) Typical Art Nouveau letters.

83) A cast of letters from the base of the Trajan column of 114 AD, in the Victoria and Albert Museum, was used as a model for teaching lettering in art schools. The Trajan inscription lacked H, J, K, U, W, Y and Z. Here U has been drawn to fit the style of the other letters. The roman capitals in Section 3 owe much to this and similar inscriptions.

84) Geometric letters from the 1930's, suitable for metal work or neon tubing and owing little to historical sources.

85) Modern sans serif letters, less geometric than (84). The sans serif capitals in Section 3 are similar to these forms.

85 M ART

ORIA

86 MCREVT

87 ameht

88 prʒebs

89 amegtr

90 abneusg

LOWERCASE

Up to the 19th Century

The development of the small letter alphabet, commonly known by the printer's term *lowercase*, followed the growth of the manuscript book in Europe. Under the influence of the broad pen the square forms of roman capitals were transformed into the round shapes more natural to writing. When printing was invented the tenth century minuscule letter was adopted in Italy as a model for text type and this style remains in general use today. During the centuries after the invention of printing, lowercase letters, like capitals (see page 60), went through changes in weight and contrast, but the basic shapes remained intact.

86) Rustic capitals, before sixth century.

87) Uncial, fifth to ninth centuries.

88) Half-uncial, fifth to ninth centuries.

89) Carolingian Minuscule, ninth to thirteenth centuries.

90) Blackletter, thirteenth to fifteenth centuries.

91) Lowercase type, fifteenth to sixteenth centuries.

91

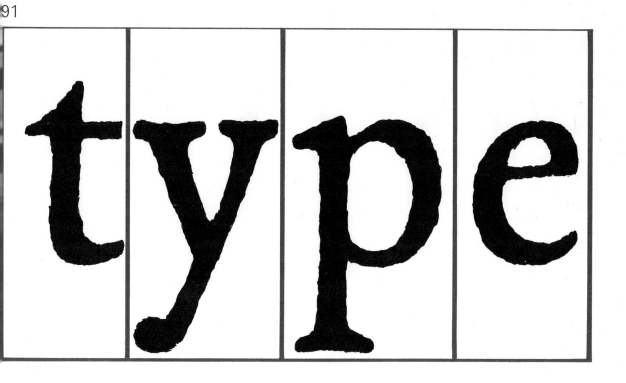

crafts

92

93 Private
Press

94 stra

At the beginning of the twentieth century Edward Johnston led a revival of broad pen calligraphy, an art which had disappeared with the spread of printed books, (see Technique 2). Book printing was revitalised by the revival of several typefaces based on historical models. In Germany a 'lowercase only' style became fashionable, where designers dispensed with capital letters altogether (see page 151).

92) Typical broad pen letters.

93) The kind of 'old face' letter revived in the first decades of this century, based on *Caslon*, a typeface first produced *c* 1725. The roman lowercase alphabet in Section 3 owes much to this letter and to the broad pen revival.

94) Eric Gill's *Perpetua*, an original twentieth century design.

95) Typical 'twenties' letters – like tubular furniture.

96) The kind of sans serif letter that is in general use today.

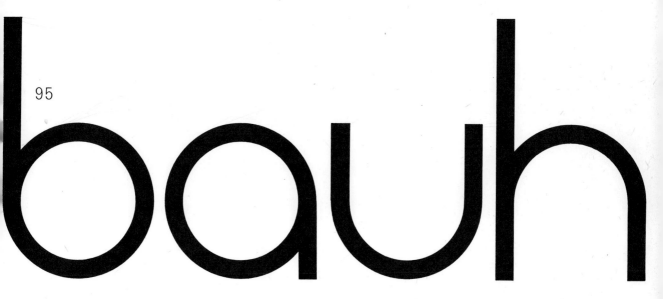

95 bauh

96 grap

Chancery Script

ITALIC

15th Century to
16th Century

The italic letterform, elegant and compressed, was often embellished with flourishes (see page 117), and the lettering of such as Arrighi, Palatino and Tagliente, who practised this style, was publicised through writing manuals printed from wood blocks. When the technique of type-founding was established in Italy this letterform became a model. The first italic types had very little slope and were used with upright capitals, although capitals with a slight slope were introduced later.

97) A drawn version of italic letters (see Technique 3 for an analysis of these forms). The italic alphabet in Section 3 is close to these letters.

98) Italic type with a roman initial. Because of its narrow form italic was often used for printing cheap books in which it was necessary to get as many words on a page as possible. Later, italic was used in roman lowercase text for emphasis and contrast, and books were rarely set entirely in italic.

98

Textu

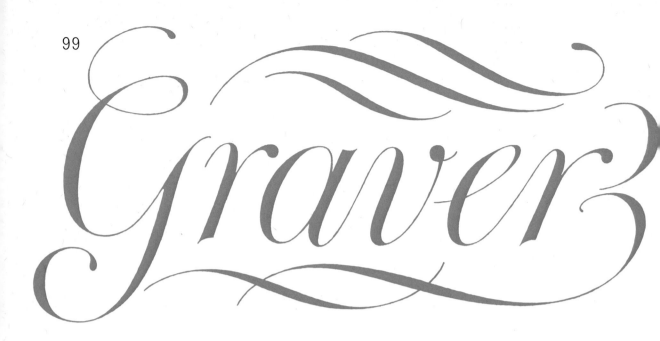

Graver

abcd
etc

ITALIC

17th Century to 19th Century

Italic continued its double life, as handwriting and a style of typeface, undergoing several changes, the most marked being an increase in its slope. The skills of the copperplate engraver found scope for display in flourished backgrounds to lettering, and the style became known as *copperplate*. Italic typefaces lost some of their pen-made characteristics; during the nineteenth century *commercial script* maintained the tradition of formal handwriting.

99) A drawn version of engraved italic script, the forms less angular than (97).

100) A late eighteenth century type design with a greater slope than (98).

101) Typical commercial script of the nineteenth century, dominated by loops and large capitals.

101 *Dear Sir,*
Oats at th
lowest market p
your invoicing t

102 *Handwr*

103 *Letters of C.S. Lewis*

ITALIC

20th Century

In this century earlier, sixteenth century, forms of italic have made a great comeback, due to the efforts of pioneers such as Alfred Fairbank, who have built on the calligraphic work of Edward Johnston and re-established it as a model for handwriting. Until art schools re-establish the teaching of lettering, italic handwriting is the only skill in this field being widely taught. Italic lettering adds distinction to many commercial purposes, including book jackets and monograms.

102) Enlarged forms of italic handwriting.

103) Monogram of interlaced capital letters. See also (135).

104) Condensed italic letters that fit well the upright rectangle of a book jacket.

105) *Palatino*, a typeface designed by Hermann Zapf in 1950.

104

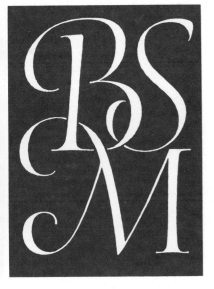

105

Palatino

FURTHER READING

Degering, Hermann, *Lettering*, Ernest Benn, 1929

Gray, Nicolete, *Lettering on Buildings*, The Architectural Press, 1960

Handover, P. M., *Letters Without Serifs*, Motif 6, 1961

McLean, Ruari, *Modern Book Design*, Faber and Faber, 1958

Morison, Stanley, *Letter Forms*, Bodley Head, 1968

    On Type Designs Past and Present, Ernest Benn, 1962

Mosley, James, *English Vernacular*, Motif II, 1964

    Trajan Revived, Alphabet, 1964

Ryder, John, *Lines of the Alphabet*, Stellar Press and Bodley Head, 1965

Sutton, James and Bartram, Alan, *An Atlas of Typeforms*, Lund Humphries, 1968

    2000 Years of Calligraphy, Frederick Muller, 1972

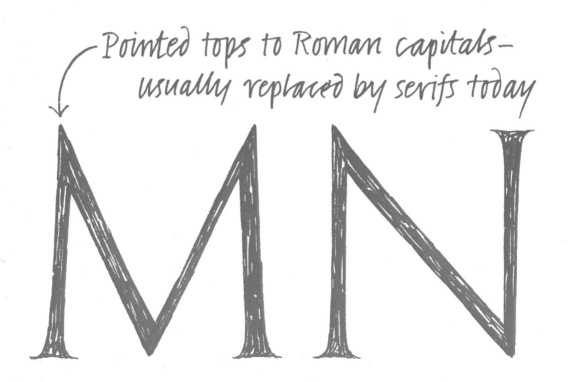

Pointed tops to Roman capitals— usually replaced by serifs today

Alphabets 3

The alphabets displayed in this section have been specially designed to provide reliable basic models, free from mannerisms and period detail. As far as possible both the roman and sans serif letters share common proportions and weight of vertical strokes, but fundamental differences of form and proportion have been kept; e.g. the open roman C and the closed sans serif C, the narrow roman E and the wide sans serif E.

Students using these alphabets for drawing practice should start by carefully tracing the letters to familiarise themselves with the shapes. Further drawing practice should follow the principles described in Section 1. Unless the student intends to become a lettering designer in his own right there is no need for his exercises to achieve a high degree of finish. The ability to get the shapes right is much more important.

These model alphabets are not intended to do more than give a good understanding of letter design. In practice many variations can and should be made.

ROMAN CAPITALS

This alphabet (shown on the following left-hand pages) is a contemporary version of roman capital letters whose historical development is outlined in Section 2. The curved letters have a vertical stress, and the serifs grow smoothly from the strokes ending in blunt points. The ratio between thick and thin strokes is approximately 4:1, and the ratio between the thick stroke and the letter-height is approximately 8:1. The proportions and optical refinements are as detailed in Section 1, with the exception that letter O and other circular letters are very slightly condensed because a fully circular form is visually disturbing in lettering designs. These roman capitals are used in (140), (149) and (166).

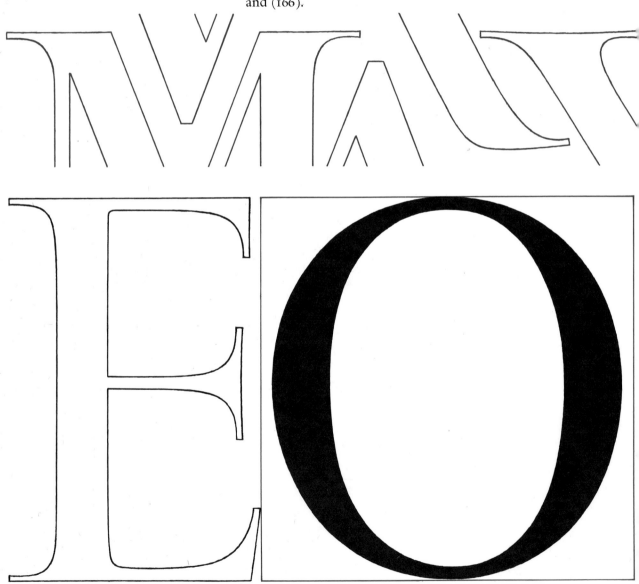

SANS SERIF CAPITALS

This alphabet (on the following right-hand pages) is an example of a modern sans serif, less geometric than earlier twentieth century versions and nearer to nineteenth century designs. The history of this style is outlined in Section 2. The stroke to letter-height ratio is approximately 8:1, making this, like the roman capitals described opposite, a medium-weight alphabet. Circular letters are based on a slightly condensed circle, otherwise the general proportions are as described in Geometry 2. Section 1 gives details of the many refinements in this apparently simple alphabet. These sans serif capitals are used in (144), (169) and (171).

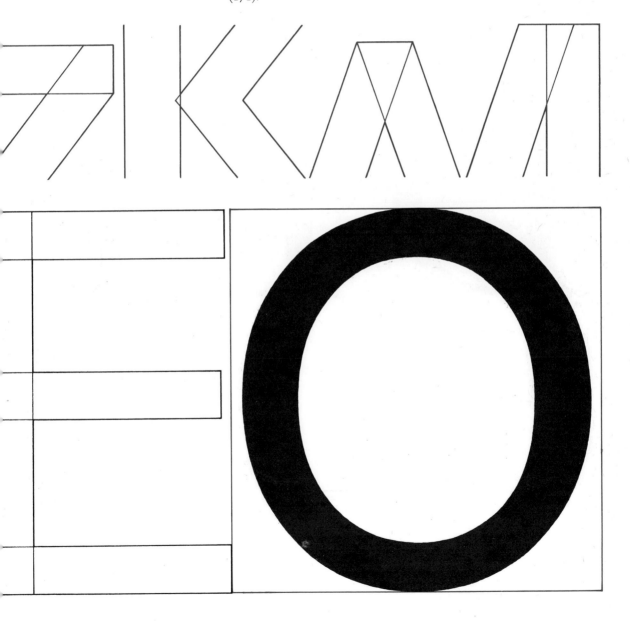

A B C

D E F

G H I J

A B C

D E F

G H I J

KLM
NOP
QRS

K L M

N O P

Q R S

TUV

WX

Y&Z

T U V
W X
Y & Z

1 2 3

4 5 6 7

8 9 0

1 2 3

4 5 6 7

8 9 0

A Q P

R R R

Y J &

ALTERNATIVE
CHARACTERS

Although the characters in the preceding alphabets are the simplest and most usual forms, several alternative forms can be used. The open form of P is often seen in Roman inscriptions; the long-tailed Q is an attractive variant where space allows (the short-tailed version is really a restriction of metal type where letters are cast on a rectangular body making extensions technically difficult); the curved tail to R is a long-standing alternative to the classic Roman form, and the simple, open R is more geometric than the others; the single-serif diagonal arms of Y echo the tail of the open R, and these two characters often appear in the same alphabets.

The variation on the ampersand shows more clearly than the usual form the origin of the character in the Latin *et*, meaning *and*.

Sans serif capitals have few alternatives to the standard forms, but this R with a curved junction of the tail is common and this ampersand is a more open form than the usual character.

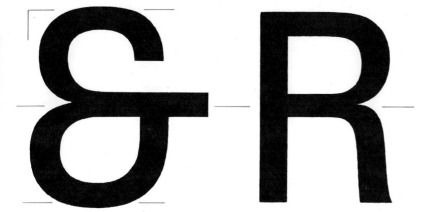

ROMAN LOWERCASE

The lowercase alphabet (on the following left-hand pages) is designed to accompany the capitals on pages 78, 80, and 82, its basic calligraphic structure (described in Technique 2) adapted to match the style of the capitals—a practice going back to early printing types. The serifs are similar in style to those of the capitals, but many letters have half serifs with a slight tilt from the horizontal (a calligraphic detail) and ascending strokes go above the capital height. Curved letters maintain a slight oblique calligraphic stress. Alternatives to serifs are shown for a, c, f, j, r and y. This alphabet is used for the title-page and section headings of this book and for (146).

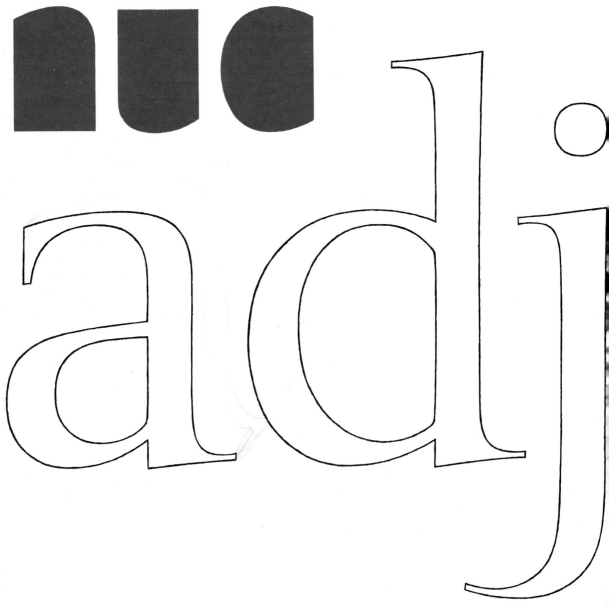

This lowercase alphabet (on the following right-hand pages), designed to accompany the capitals on pages 79, 81, and 83, is similar in proportion to the roman lowercase described opposite, but a, c, e and s are less open. The g is a different shape to the roman g and the ascending strokes do not go above the capitals. The dots over i and j are round; square dots can be used as an alternative. This alphabet is used in (147) and (191).

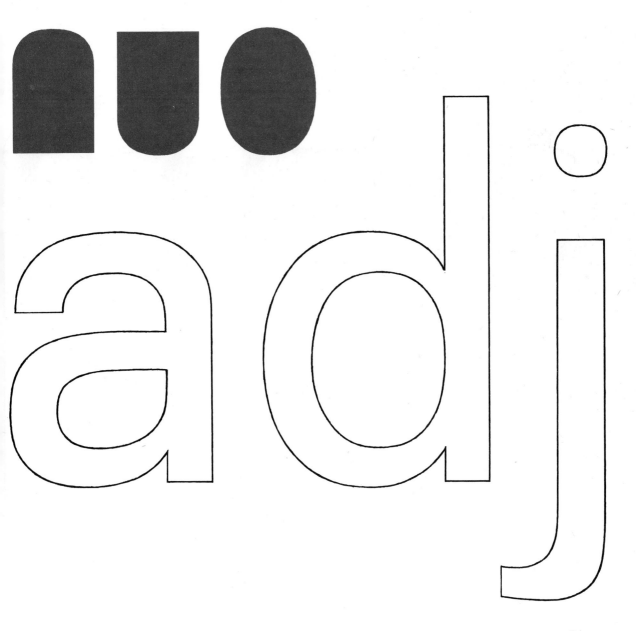

abcd

efghij

klmn

abcd

efghij

klmn

opqrs
tuvw
xyz

opqrs

tuvw

xyz

1 2 3 4 5

6 7 8 9

! ? £ $. ,

NON-RANGING FIGURES & OTHER CHARACTERS

The figures shown left are designed to accompany roman lowercase letters. These 'old style' figures were usual in early typefaces and remain in use today. The even-height figures shown on page 84 are a relatively modern development. Figures in sans serif typefaces are usually capital height, as shown on page 85, but a useful set of non-ranging figures are included here. In both non-ranging styles a lowercase o is used for zero.

Alphabet families include several non-letter characters and various punctuation marks designed to fit the general style. The most common in roman and sans serif are shown here.

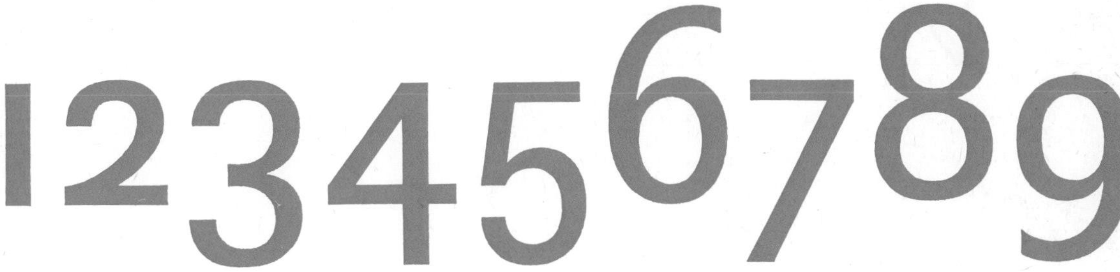

123456789

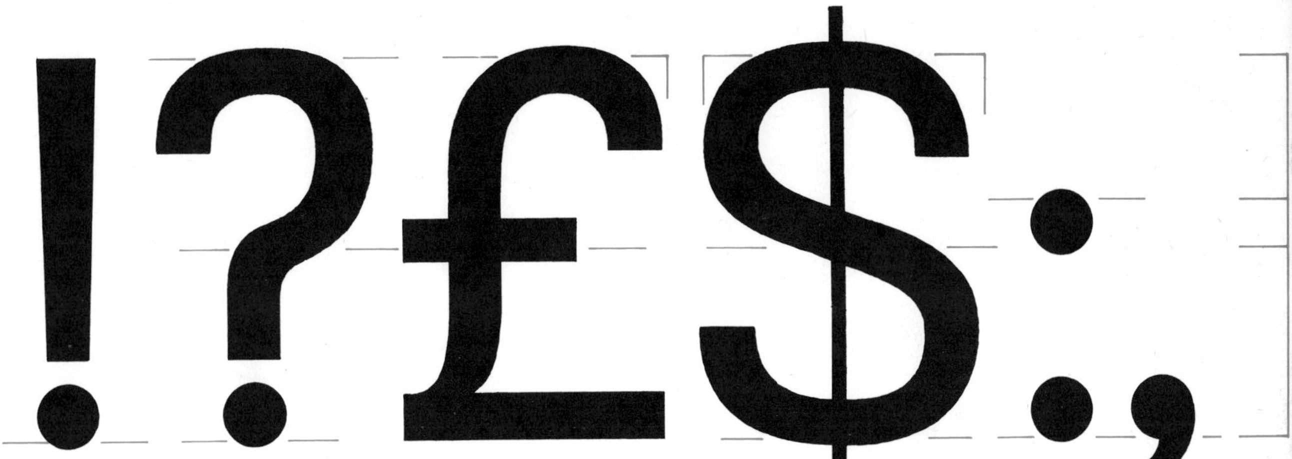

!?£$;,

ITALIC

This formal script letter (on the following left-hand pages), whose calligraphic basis is shown in Technique 3, is complementary to the roman capital and lowercase alphabets already illustrated, but has its own sloping capital letters. Some of these, which essentially are sloping versions of roman capitals, are shown on page 102. The history of this italic letter is outlined in Section 2. Serifs are quite steeply angled and give the letter some of its flowing quality, and the ascending strokes reach above the capital height. In weight the letters match the roman lowercase letters, having the same x-height and stroke thickness. The angle of slope is 10 degrees.

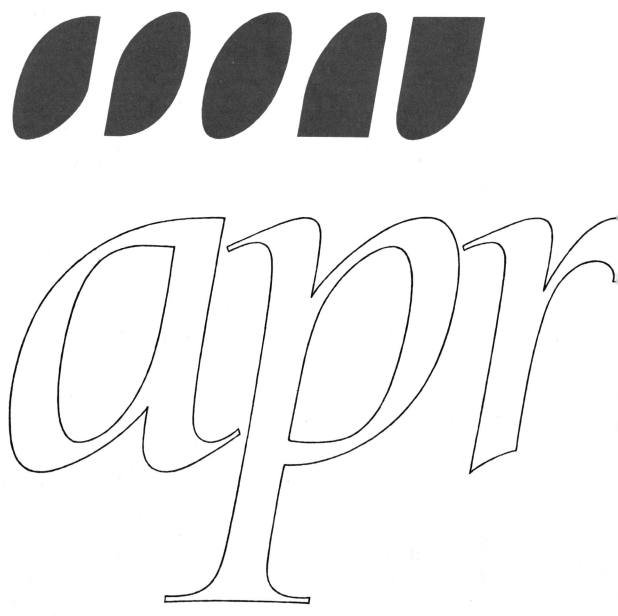

SANS SERIF ITALIC

This letter (on the following right-hand pages) is not a script but a sloped version of the sans serif lowercase alphabet, having the same weight and x-height. Sloping capitals are used, some of which are shown on page 103. The information given on sloping letters in Geometry 4 and 5, applies particularly to this alphabet. The angle of slope is 10 degrees. This alphabet is used in (170).

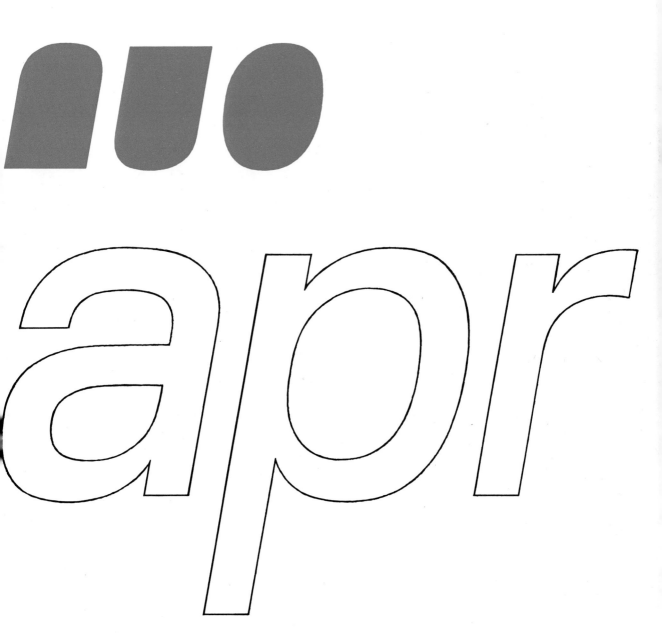

97

abcd

efghij

klmn

abcd

efghij

klmn

opqrs

tuvw

xyz

opqrs

tuvw

xyz

&BC

KRS

QUX

&BC

KRS

QUX

FURTHER READING

Gill, Eric, *An Essay on Typography*, J. M. Dent & Sons, 1931

Leach, Mortimer, *Lettering for Advertising*, Reinhold, 1956

Lindgren, Erik, *ABC of Lettering and Printing types*, Erik Lindgren Grafisk Studio, 1964

Tschichold, Jan, *Treasury of Alphabets and Lettering*, Reinhold, 1966

Zapf, Hermann, *Pen and Graver*, Museum Books, 1952

Victoria & Albert Museum, *Roman Lettering*, *A Book of Alphabets and Inscriptions*, H. M. Stationery Office, 1958

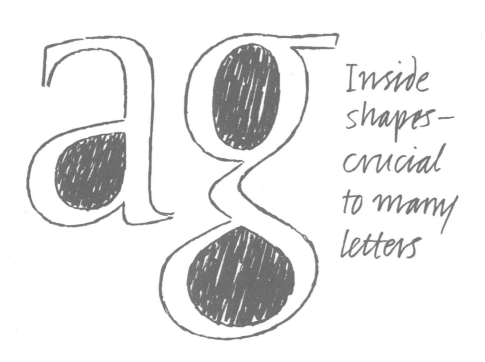

Inside shapes—crucial to many letters

Variations 4

The alphabets illustrated in Section 3 are standard letter designs of normal weight and proportions, but many variations on these standard forms are possible to make a greatly increased range of letterforms. In describing the main areas where variations can be made, it is inevitable that some overlap will occur. However, it is important to establish clear definitions, and the principles outlined apply to many alphabets, and not only to the lettering illustrated in this book. It is the purpose of this section to make the student aware of the wealth of letterforms available to the designer through a study of particular and representative design variations.

Students should experiment for themselves, using the alphabets in Section 3 as a basis for the variations described on the following pages.

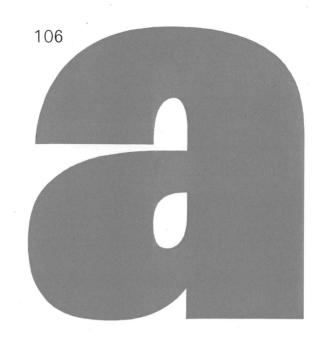

ELEG

THE BODLEY HEAD

The strokes of letterforms can be made thinner or thicker than normal to produce light and bold versions of the standard forms. These variations in weight can be taken furthest in sans serif letters. In very bold letters a monolithic sculptural quality replaces the open strokes of lighter forms.

106) A very bold sans serif lowercase a in which the strokes become solid areas. In extreme examples of this kind the counters (the inside shapes of letters) should be kept as open as possible. See also (118), (175) and (179).

107) Light sans serif capitals, with pointed apexes to A and N. See also (84) and (174).

108) Bold roman capitals; the serifs are enlarged and in E the top and bottom horizontals are lengthened to make room for the middle serif. See also (23), (77), (79), (156), (168), (193) and (194).

109) Bold roman lowercase with a strong sculptural quality.

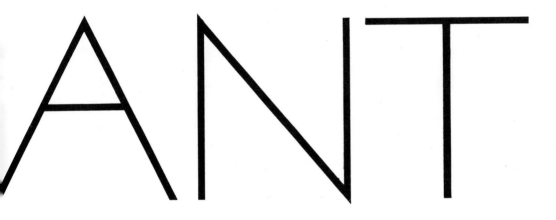

109

110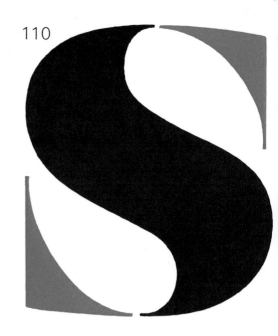

111 KNIFE

113 str

The degree of contrast between thick and thin strokes in roman alphabets can be increased or decreased.

110) An extreme example in which the thin strokes are broken. The serifs are greatly enlarged to counterbalance the weight of the main stroke, a normal requirement in letters with a strong contrast. See also (79), (136) and (174).

111) Roman capitals less extreme than (110). The serifs, enlarged to compensate for loss of weight in the thin hair-line strokes, introduce strong curves in normally rectangular letters. F and E are wider than normal to make room for the larger serifs. See also (78) and (79).

112) Roman capitals with minimum contrast, reminiscent of early inscriptional forms. The serifs are not very pronounced. See also (61), (72), (164) and (197).

113) Lowercase letters with strong contrast emphasising the calligraphic stress of the curved strokes. See (51) and (92).

112

MONDAY DATE

etch

114 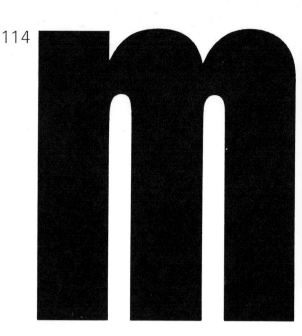m

115 vogue

116 BAR

The geometric basis of the proportions of letters can be condensed or extended. In an alphabet the same degree of proportional change should be maintained throughout. The degree to which such changes are possible will depend on the style of letter; sans serif letters, with their relatively simple construction, can be condensed or extended considerably, but roman letters are less flexible, see (168). Junctions and curved strokes will need modification. See Geometry 3 and 6, and Optics 4.

114) Very condensed sans serif lowercase m; such letters are strong shapes, but the near loss of essential characteristics, such as curves, tends to make them illegible. See also (31) and (179).

115) Condensed roman lowercase letters with short descender on g have a vertical emphasis.

116) Extended roman capitals; generous open forms with long serifs, including a serif on the top of A which helps to maintain alignment. See also (176).

117) Extended sans serif capitals.

118) Less extreme and more legible than (114).

117

FACADE

118

blues

119

120
STRONG

121
sea
sport

CURVES

Round to Square

The strength and unity of letters can be greatly increased by flattening the curved strokes to lessen the differences between round and square characters.

119) An extreme example in which rounded corners are all that remain of the curved stroke; separation of the curve from the vertical and mechanical drawing emphasise the letter's angularity. See also (183) and (195).

120) Almost serif-less roman capitals with little contrast are strengthened by squared curves. Compare with (112).

121) The round forms of roman lowercase are given a chunky quality, emphasised by minimum spacing.

122) Italic letters, squarer and more condensed than normal. See also (103), (172) and (177).

123) A more subtle design than (119). Compare with (143) and (150).

Blackletter forms (90) are an extreme example of straight and bent strokes replacing curves.

122

Decoratior

123

BOSS

124 125 126 127

128

129 130 131

SERIFS

A Variety of Styles

Serifs vary in design to suit particular styles of letter.

124) An embryo serif; the stroke swells slightly and has a concave end. See (160), (164) and (197).

125) Bold slab serif. See (79), (156) and (183).

126) Split serif. See (80).

127) Very fine serif, without brackets, reminiscent of engraving.

128) Strong but elegant serif with swelling, rounded ends.

129) Rounded serif, which easily declines into a shapeless blob.

130) Very concave generous serif with fine curved ends. See (135).

131) Half serif, characteristic of the lead-in stroke in brush drawn letters. See (173) and (177).

In general serifs should be an integral part of letters, and not give the appearance of having been stuck on as an afterthought.

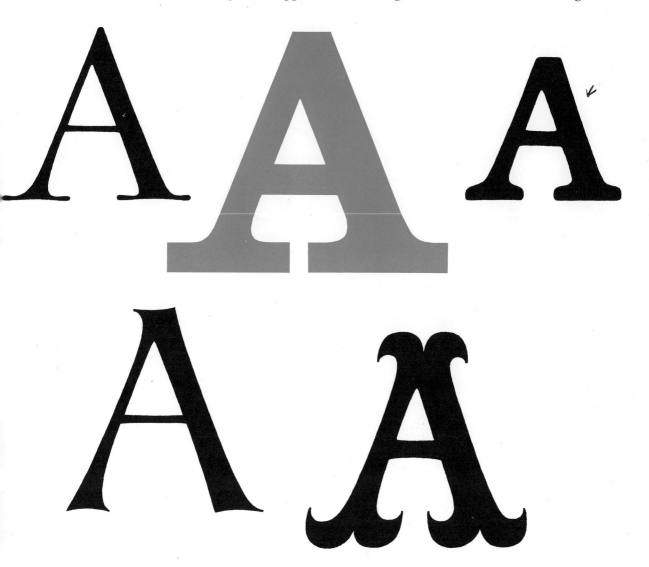

132

F

133

ABEF
GHJKN
RTVYZ

FLOURISHES

Swash Letters

Many of the variations described in this section are applicable to italic letters (except that this essentially narrow letter should not be made any wider), but this is the only letterform that lends itself to calligraphic flourishing.

132) Capital F with flourished horizontal and vertical strokes. This is called a 'swash' letter.

133) Typical 'swash' capitals. Often used as initial letters they can be used together, particularly for monograms. See also (104) and (159).

134) The ascenders and descenders of italic lowercase lend themselves to this elegant treatment. Likewise the r where space allows. See also (97) and (99).

135) Capital letters whose flourishes intertwine.

Many good examples of flourished letters can be found in sixteenth century writing manuals, several facsimiles of which are listed at the end of this section. When drawing flourishes it is important to remember their calligraphic origins and follow the angled pen's formation of thick and thin strokes. See Technique 2 and 3.

134

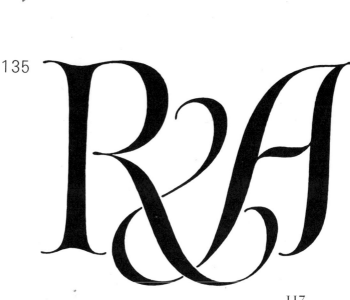

135

136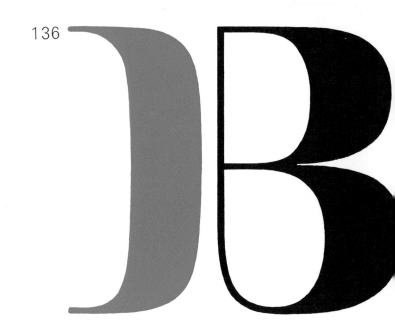

137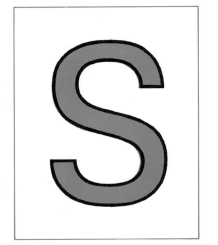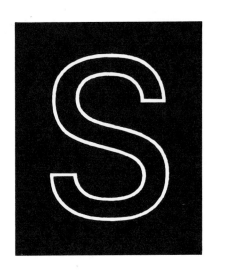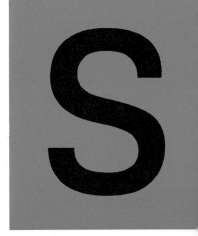

GRAPHICS

Invention and Variety

Graphic inventiveness can give letter shapes a new interest by a re-interpretation of the usual forms. The stencil treatment shown in (119) is an example. Colour and outline can also extend a letter's effectiveness.

136) A capital letter with strong contrast given a new twist by the combination of thick and thin strokes in the vertical. Colour emphasises this effect.

137) A letter can be represented in a variety of ways: a solid, black on white or colour; drawn in outline; filled with colour; the outline reversed with or without a coloured centre. The graphic variations open to the designer are very wide and should be fully exploited.

138) The use of shadow on letters is a long-standing graphic device. In this example the letters touch with a very deliberate joining of the R to the A. It is important that joined letters should retain their identities. See also (18), (70), (71), (73), (182) and (196).

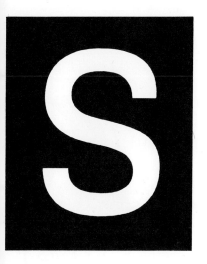 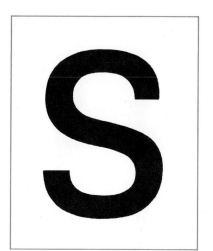 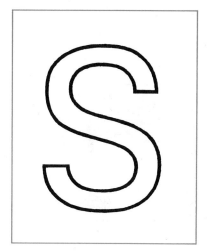

138

TIARA

FURTHER READING

Cresci, Francesco Giovan, *Essemplare, 1578*, (Fascimile), Bodley Head, 1968

Da Carpi, Ugo, *Thesauro de Scrittori, 1535*, (Facsimile), Bodley Head, 1968

De Yciar, Juan, *Arte Subtilissima, 1550*, (Facsimile), Oxford University Press, 1960

Fairbank, Alfred and Wolpe, Berthold, *Renaissance Handwriting*, Faber and Faber, 1960

Gray, Nicolete, *Lettering as Drawing*, Oxford University Press, 1971

Haab, Armin, *Lettera 1, 2, 3 and 4*, Arthur Niggli, 1954–1972

Kelly, Rob Roy, *American Wood Type 1828–1900*, Van Nostrand Reinhold, 1969

Lambert, Frederick, *Letter Forms*, Peter Owen, 1964

Ogg, Oscar, *Three Centuries Of Italian Calligraphy*, (Facsimile), Dover Publications, 1953

Vincent Figgins Type Specimens 1801 & 1815, (Facsimile), Printing Historical Society, 1967

Weinberger, Norman, *Encyclopedia of Comparative Letterforms*, Art Direction Book Co., 1971

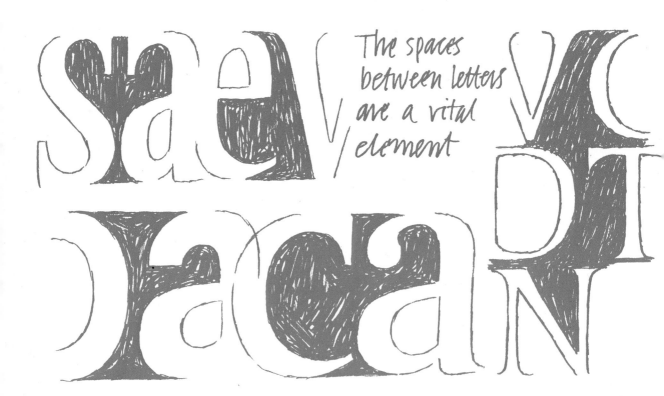

The spaces between letters are a vital element

Letters into Words 5

Letters are single forms which only function when they are combined to make words; these make lines and lines are arranged to make the final architecture of lettering. In this section the principles of this organisation are given stage by stage, presenting a clear idea of the relationship between a complete design and its parts.

Two major principles emerge from these pages. The first is legibility. This prerequisite of the majority of good lettering design is here given a special emphasis, since it is sometimes lacking in current practice. The other principle is the great decorative value of letterforms; good design should recognise and exploit this potential.

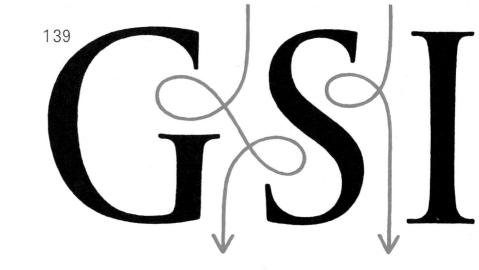

139

140

CLASSIC

141

WOMEN

142

CHARTER

SPACING CAPITALS
Roman and Sans Serif

The spacing of letters is a vital element in the organisation of letters into words and needs as much attention as the letters themselves. The basic facts about letter spacing have been given in Optics 5.

139) Space is the element which flows around and between letters and it follows that unless sufficient distance is left between letters this flow will be impeded. This space-flow principle is illustrated here.

140) Roman capitals benefit from generous spacing. See (83).

141) The occurrence of thin strokes in these letters allows for closer spacing than shown in (140). See (78).

142) Condensed letters require minimum spacing consistent with legibility, and serifs may touch if necessary. See (168).

143) Condensed flat-sided sans serif letters can have minimum spacing, but large spaces occur between certain letters.

144) Sans serif letters do not require generous spacing and are best set fairly close together. See (35).

143

PUBLICITY

144

NOTICE

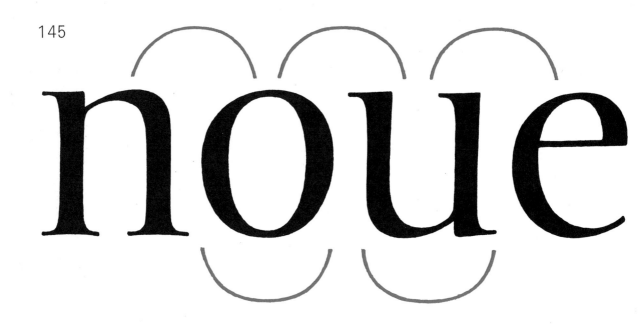

noue

Illuminate

Illuminate

Illumina

SPACING LOWERCASE

Roman and Sans Serif

The spacing of lowercase letters is comparatively simple as there are fewer different forms than in capital letters.

145) The round forms of these letters and the spaces between are like the links in a chain. If the spacing is too tight adjacent vertical strokes merge together, making an uneven word pattern. Conversely, if the letters are over-spaced the links in the chain will be broken and the word's unity destroyed.

146) Three examples in roman lowercase. The middle word is correctly spaced, the top word is too closely set and the bottom word is over-spaced.

147) The lack of serifs should not be an excuse to pack sans serif letters too closely together, or solid areas will occur where several vertical strokes coincide.

148) Correct spacing of sans serif lowercase.

147

medallist

148

unive

149

RESS MESSEN

ALL THE WA

150

CIAL DELIVER

AT SENDER'S

151

ONE TWO THREE
FOUR FIVE SIX
SEVEN EIGHT NINE

As letters need spacing to produce even, legible word units, so words need spacing to produce good lines, and good inter-line spacing is necessary if a text is to be legible and attractive. The spaces between words need to be the minimum which will distinguish one word from the next, and this space should take into account the shapes of the final and initial letters in both words. Wider spacing will tend to break up the flow of the line. Word spacing should also take into account the amount of letter spacing used in the words. The spaces between lines need to be at least enough to stop the eye of the reader from jumping lines, but can be increased for visual effect.

149) Roman capitals, well spaced, with related word and line spacing.

150) Condensed sans serif capitals, with minimum letter, word and line spacing.

151) The bad practice of spacing words to fit an arbitrary measure, which, when combined with minimal line spacing, causes the text to read vertically instead of horizontally.

152) Lowercase letters need extra line spacing to avoid collisions between ascenders and descenders, although with drawn lettering quite close line spacing can be achieved. See also (163) and (167).

In all lettering work it is essential that the spacing throughout should be as consistent as possible and not arbitrarily varied.

152

Le quattr
Vivaldi

153

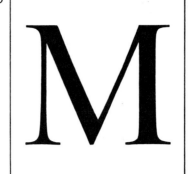

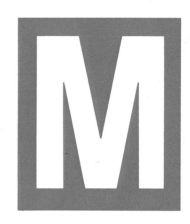

154

A SURVEY
OF THE
CHEMICAL
INDUSTRY
IN THE
MIDLANDS

155

A SURVEY
OF THE
CHEMICAL
INDUSTRY
IN THE
MIDLANDS

MARGINS

Lettering and Background

Lettering has a background and its relationship to this is determined by the margins, which will in turn be determined by the amount of letter, word and line spacing employed.

153) The open space of the roman capital requires wider margins than the bold sans serif letter.

154) A symmetrical arrangement with generous margins.

155) The same arrangement with cramped margins. These should never be less than the word and line spaces.

156) Minimum margins for a close arrangement of capitals with generous line spacing.

SEE OVERLEAF

157) The asymmetrical form of capital F requires a larger margin on the left and a smaller margin on the right. Compare with (153).

158) A spacious asymmetrical arrangement of capitals with generous margins. Compare with (154).

159) A flourished initial needs generous margins.

160) Closely packed bold capitals with small margins.

161) Close texture of lowercase lettering with wide margins.

162) The irregular shape of these numerals needs to be carefully placed on the background to achieve a satisfactory unity.

156

STAGE
AND FILM
REVIEW

157

F

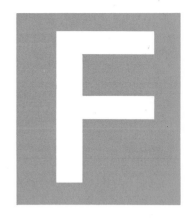

158

A SURVEY
OF THE
CHEMICAL
INDUSTRY
IN THE
MIDLANDS

159

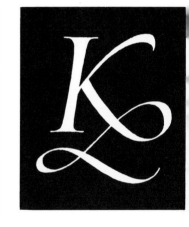

160

THE FIRST WORLD WAR A RECORD IN WORDS & PICTURES PART FIVE

161

John William Alfred Herbert Peter Sidney Mark George James Ian

162

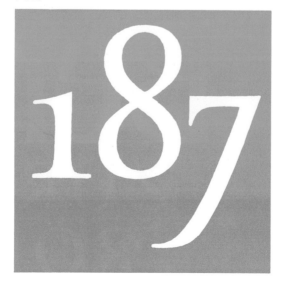

187

163

Paris
London
Berlin
Zürich
Rome

164

E·PARIS·LONDON

165

PARIS
LONDON
Berlin
ZURICH
ROME

The overall effectiveness of lettering depends on its shape and pattern, which, as long as a degree of legibility is maintained, can be very varied. Letters are only a beginning; it is their final arrangement that is of the greatest importance. The designer should be aware of the sheer decorative possibilities of even the most conventional letterforms. See (108), (121), (150), (156), (160), (161), (168), (172), (173) and (197).

163) A well integrated pattern of lowercase letters.

164) A simple, majestic frieze of capitals.

165) A large word in lowercase between lines of capitals.

166) An asymmetrical arrangement of capitals makes a distinctive and lively pattern.

In the choice of word pattern the designer needs to consider several factors, not the least being the meaning of the text. These factors are outlined in Section 6.

BERLIN·ZURICH·P

166 PARIS

LONDON

BERLIN

ZURICH

ROME

Early
English
Silver
Ware

167

Early
English
Silver
Ware

The designer's control over the spacing and fit of letters is limited when type is used, but is increased with the use of film or transfer letters, and greatly increased with drawn lettering.

167) The coincidence of ascenders and descenders in typeset lowercase letters can be mitigated by slightly condensing the first word and extending the second, shortening the ascenders and descenders and using smaller capitals. As there are no ascenders or descenders between the third and fourth lines the line-space is reduced to improve the unity of the word pattern.

168) This typeset title has some ugly letter-spaces, but careful drawing can minimise these flaws and improve the overall consistency of the letter-pattern.

Although both examples shown here are drawn a designer has considerable scope in achieving similar results by modifying film or transfer letters. Careful lengthening or shortening of serifs can improve spacing, and letters can be cut up and re-assembled to increase or decrease word width.

HEAVY
INDUSTRY
TODAY

168

HEAVY INDUSTRY TODAY

A REVIEW OF CHILDREN'S BOOKS

A review of children's books

A REVIEW OF CHILDREN'S BOOKS

The final shape that lettering design makes will depend on words which vary in length. Avoid arrangements in which dominant shapes occur, particularly rectangles and triangles, which may unbalance the overall shape. Lettering should not be forced into arbitrary shapes but should seek the most suitable arrangement of the words. Learn to recognise and subtly emphasize these word patterns.

169) Slight changes in spacing will remove the block effect of the second and third lines.

170) A long line followed by a single word is unbalanced; a more satisfactory result can be achieved by re-arranging the words.

171) This ugly 'step' arrangement should be avoided if possible.

172) Smaller and more condensed letters shorten the top line. This is an improvement on the arrangement in (171).

172

A review of children's books

173

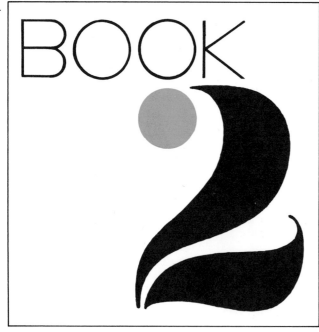

GOSPEL MUSIC

174

BOOK 2

175

Newsagent

26

176

SMITH & SONS
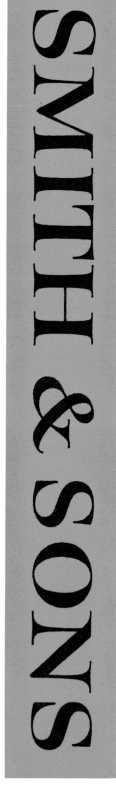

Most lettering has to be designed to fit a given shape, and the designer has to find the best way to achieve this. Five typical layout problems and alternative solutions are shown here.

173) Letters fill this square with a free and vigorous pattern. See also (160).

174) Letters and a large numeral are placed in a precise, asymmetrical relationship within the square. Space is a positive part of this design.

175) Lettering on a shop fascia uses a condensed letter to create a space between the name and the numeral.

176) Expanded letters fill this shop fascia.

177) Three ways to design lettering to run across the spine of a book. The author in two lines of capitals, and the title in bold italics with a flourished tail to the y; the author and title in lowercase, with the y making a decorative effect in both cases; two sizes of capitals for the title and lowercase for the author.

In any design problem several layouts should be tried, using various combinations of letters. An effective simplicity should be the aim of the designer.

177

April price and stock list **RS** from Ross and Smith Ltd

EARLS COURT
JUNE 3–16

book fair

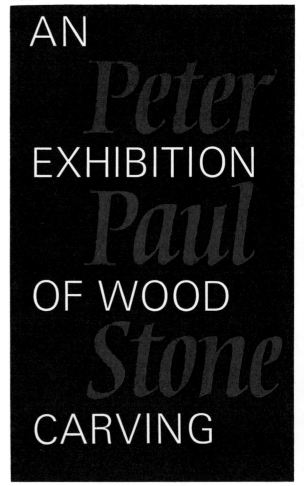

AN *Peter* EXHIBITION *Paul* OF WOOD *Stone* CARVING

In combining one style of letter with another the aim is to achieve dramatic contrast and definition within a design. Two similar but different letter styles, two scripts for instance, should not be used together, but two very dissimilar styles can often be joined in a successful marriage, particularly if a contrast in scale is used. The designer of lettering will find much scope here for the exercise of visual judgement and imagination.

178) Plain sans serif letters contrast well with drawn initials.
179) Large, bold sans serif lowercase letters, making a strong vertical pattern, with two lines of well spaced roman capitals.
180) Large-scale italic alternating with light sans serif capitals.
181) Italic letters contrast with lowercase in the same line, and the colour emphasises the contrast.
182) The thick and thin outline of the initial is complemented by the thick and thin strokes of the accompanying capitals.
183) Bold, square slab-serif capitals contrast with roman capitals.

181

*the*wine*shop*

182

183

B

BOND
&
SONS

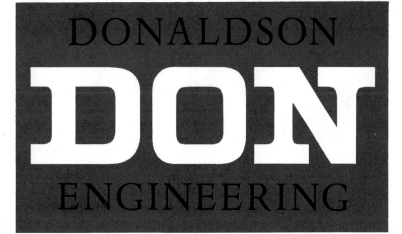

DONALDSON
DON
ENGINEERING

FURTHER READING

Ballinger, Raymond A., *Sign, Symbol and Form*, Reinhold, 1973
Brinkley, John, *Lettering Today*, Studio Vista, 1964
Bradshaw, Christopher, *Design*, Vista Books, 1964
Child, Heather, *Calligraphy Today*, Studio Books, 1963
Dair, Carl, *Design with Type*, University of Toronto Press, 1967
Gray, Milner and Armstrong, Ronald, *Lettering for Architects and Designers*, Batsford, 1962
Morison, Stanley & Day, Kenneth, *The Typographic Book*, Ernest Benn, 1963
Shahn, Ben, *Love and Joy About Letters*, Cory, Adams and Mackay, 1964
Sutton, James, *Signs in Action*, Studio Vista, 1965
Tschichold, Jan, *Asymmetric Typography*, Faber and Faber, 1967
Zapf, Hermann, *Typographic Variations*, Museum Books, 1964

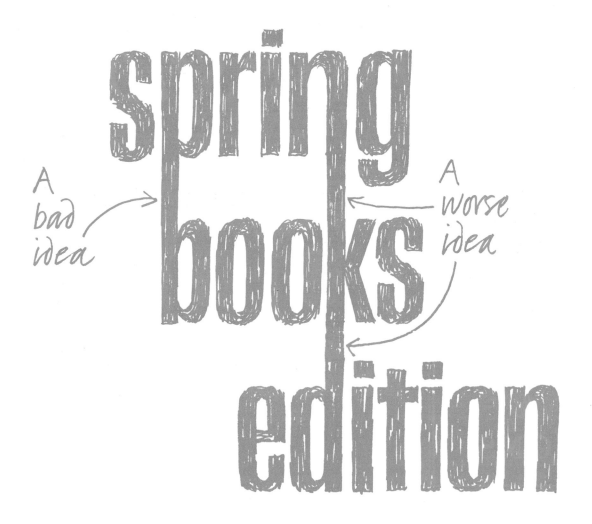

Letters at Work 6

The analysis and principles given in this book have lacked one vital element: the consideration of reality. Reality is the world outside the studio, and the designer must learn to understand its needs.

He should not be condescending, neither should he be subservient. The world has points of view which must be considered, and the designer has to learn that every design is a collaboration between client and designer, each contributing his special knowledge and skills.

In this section various aspects of lettering at work are discussed in general terms, under headings which pinpoint areas of particular importance. The philosophy of design which emerges is, I hope, both realistic and stimulating.

Heading

TITLE text

COPY

Chapter

words

PARAGRAPH sub-title

LANGUAGE

The First Consideration

It must never be forgotten that the primary purpose of most lettering is to be read, and that the visual patterns of letterforms must not be allowed to obscure this purpose.

Display lettering, which has to attract, may employ any suitable graphic means while it retains a reasonable degree of legibility, and should be intelligently organised as necessary into main and subsidiary parts (184).

Text lettering should respect the use of paragraphs, with all but the first being indented. The alternatives of an extra line space to separate paragraphs, and the old practice of placing the first letter of a paragraph into the margin, are also recommended. Commonsense should be used in breaks at line-ends, e.g. left wing/student not left/wing student.

Punctuation (185) should follow normal practice, but it is best to reduce this to a minimum in display lettering. Commas can be replaced by centred dots (164) or by oblique strokes, and the usual full point at the end of a sentence can be dispensed with if nothing follows it. The use of a full point after a title should never be necessary.

Before any design work is started the text should be read and analysed. Trial layouts should be made in order to explore the various possibilities and to determine the likely extent of the lettering. Only when this preliminary work is completed can the designer safely consider lettering styles and reach for his box of colours.

85

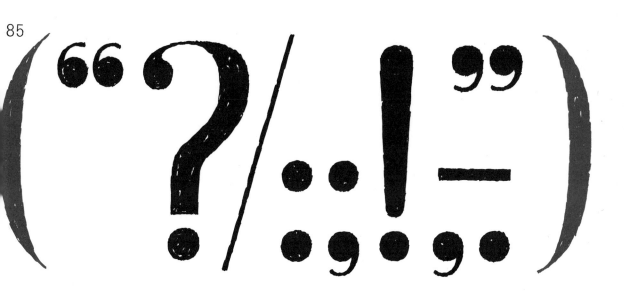

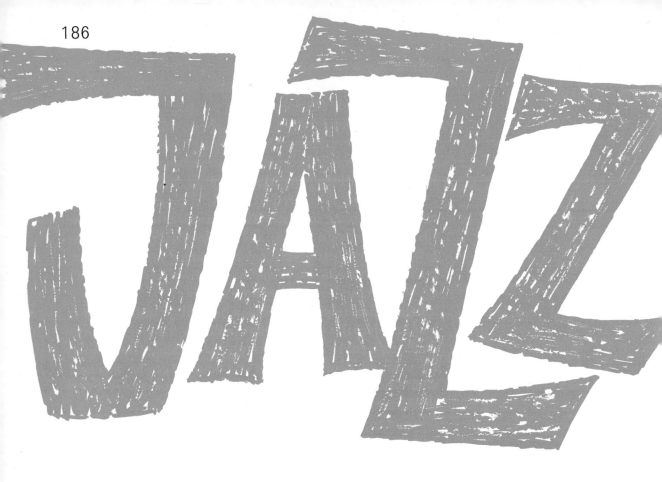

186

187

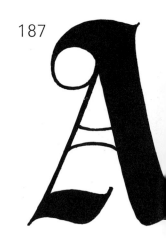

EXPRESSION

Form, Drawing and Style

Words are the starting point in lettering design, and the choice of letterform can enrich their meaning. The expressive quality of letters falls into two categories, the first being the abstract graphic qualities of weight, outline, pattern and the quality of drawing used in their making, which can add visual impact to words and strengthen their appeal. A free, vital letterform certainly expresses the driving force and individual quality of certain kinds of jazz music (186). This is a letter with no historical associations, obeying no formal rules, which invents its own patterns as a jazz musician improvises on a theme. See also (107), (120), (123) and (189).

In the second kind of approach (187) the old-fashioned feeling of the word is expressed by using a letterform which is no longer in everyday use and is felt to be a cosy embodiment of the past – rather like a mock-Tudor house. The use of archaic letterforms is a natural outcome of our knowledge of the past, and the only requirement is that they should be used with flair and precision. The designer is like an actor who must learn to play many parts and wear many costumes. See also (140) and (167).

A combination of these two approaches can produce extra richness; the way that an historical form is drawn can enhance its effectiveness and prevent a lifeless imitation. For instance, the rough drawing of (186) can be applied to (187) to increase its expressive power. Needless to say, these examples are not the only kinds of letter that can produce these effects, and these two extreme types of expression ignore the possibilities of a more subtle, allusive use of letterforms. Nevertheless, the designer should be aware of the great potential of letterforms in increasing the effectiveness of a word or message.

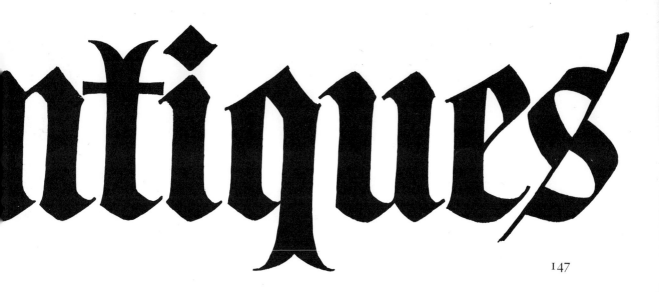

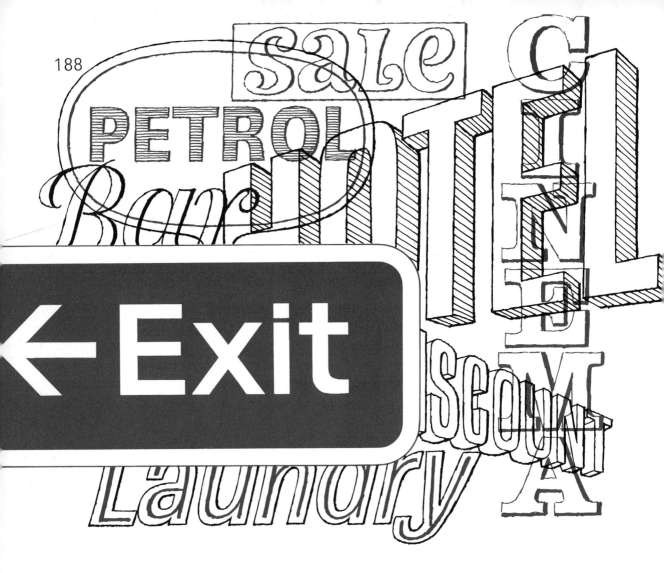

188

sale

PETROL

Bar

HOTEL

← Exit

DISCOUNT

Laundry

CINEMA

189 PLAIN

CONTEXT

Environment and Competition

The designer at his drawing-board must never forget the purpose of his work and the setting for which it is being planned. This context is of the greatest importance, for unless the questions 'who will read this?', 'where?', and 'under what conditions?' are taken into account at an early stage, the design will have no basis in reality and be ineffective.

An example of a context in its widest sense is the typical city centre with its jungle of competing signs, in which any directional sign will need to be planned with careful thought if it is to stand out against its background (188). Here the sign uses a plain sans serif letter, white on a generous background of colour, with a white frame to further isolate it from the other lettering in the street. Problems of this kind will test the designer's visual judgement and self-discipline to the utmost, and will not allow the use of letterforms for their own sake.

Another field in which the designer must consider carefully the environment is that of commercial competition. This includes posters, packaging, book jackets, shop fascias and logotypes. Here there is great scope for individuality, for the designer is making an effort to steal the limelight. Designs that are to be successful in this context will rely mainly on effecting a contrast with the competition. Where plain lettering predominates, a decorative, fancy letterform will have strong appeal, and vice versa (189).

Colour, changes in weight and proportion, the use of form and space to achieve contrast and variety, are all at the designer's disposal, weapons to be used with style, intelligence and conviction. In this field the designer needs to be well armed.

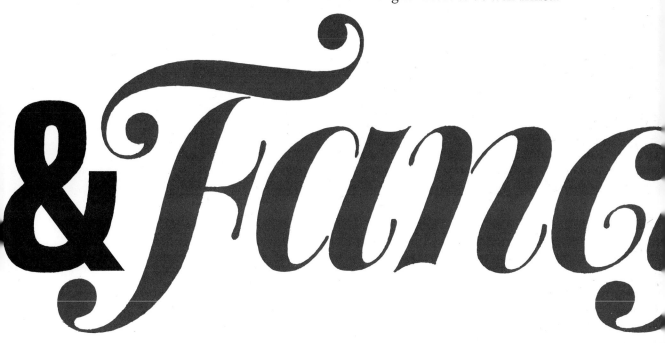

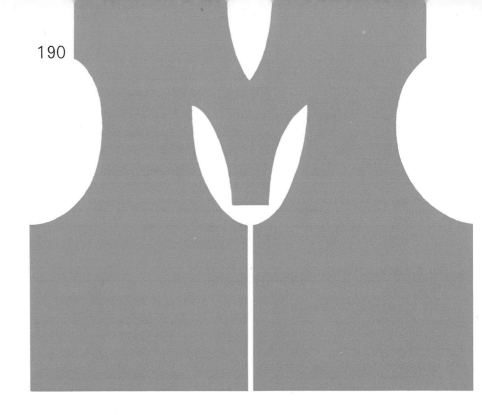

john

Faced with the bewildering and attractive array of available letter styles, the designer must learn to keep his head. Fashion is a thing of the moment, or of the past (since most fashions are subject to periodic revival), and nothing looks more dated than yesterday's styles. This applies as much to letterforms as it does to clothes. It follows that, while he should be aware of fashion, the designer should not be too eager to embrace the latest oddity to appear on the scene. In his choice of letterforms, he should remember that few occasions call for fancy dress, and jokes (190) pall with repetition.

Fashion, and the competition that feeds it, will sometimes produce alphabets of lasting value which will become useful additions to the repertoire of letterforms. The inventiveness stimulated by fashion can have a good effect on letterform design preventing the tendencies to stagnation in any art with long traditions.

The understandable frivolity of 'novelty' letterforms is not the only aspect of fashion to concern the designer. There are also ideological fashions whose influence can be much longer lived, like the 20's doctrine of dispensing with capital letters (191), and the recent fashion, resulting from the spread of film-set and transfer lettering, for ever closer setting of letters – a cult in which legibility has suffered considerably. See (146) and (147). Rigid principles of layout, in which the useful 'grid' system of typographical organisation is used in a restrictive manner denying the freedom of organic design, are a similar fashion which has acquired a certain intellectual following. Good designers will use what is helpful in current practice, but must remember that each problem is unique and cannot be solved by the application of a formula, however 'modern' the result may appear.

brown

192

193

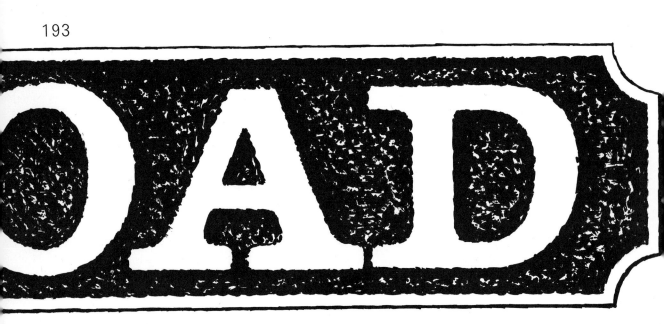

Blackletter (192), although attractive, is not a traditional letter. Tradition implies survival, and this letter died with the Renaissance, although it is still seen on the mastheads of certain newspapers, the signboards of antique shops and headings to legal documents. The roman and sans serif alphabets and their variations are the truly traditional forms that are the backbone of contemporary lettering design.

In practice the designer encounters many forms of traditional lettering and design, and has to decide if the tradition is worth maintaining or if it is redundant and needs replacing by new forms. He must decide on a policy of either renovation or innovation. An example of good traditional lettering design is to be seen in certain old street name-plates, usually cast-iron versions of roman capitals from the eighteenth and early nineteenth century (193). These robust forms could well be adapted for use on modern street name-plates (194) instead of the thin neoclassical capitals being erected everywhere, examples of official 'good taste' ignoring the excellent traditional models.

Another form of tradition is that established by commercial trademarks, magazine or newspaper mastheads, publishers' house styles, etc. In these cases the designer may have to work within well established and familiar traditions. His job will be to improve the existing forms and to avoid radical change.

In the handling of traditional or historical letterforms the spirit of the original must be respected, but at the same time slavish imitation should be avoided. A direct adaptation to modern needs will produce the most acceptable results.

194

CITY

195

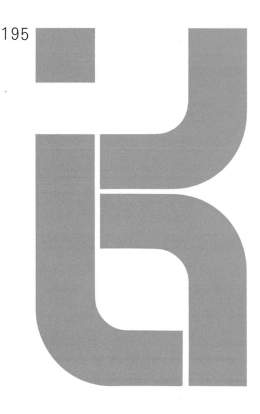

196

STUD

MONOGRAMS & LOGOTYPES

Individuality in Design

Monograms are combinations of initial letters. Logotypes are designs in which the combination of word and letterform is unique, as in a trademark or newspaper masthead. In both cases the design will, with time, become synonymous with the individual or organisation for which it stands. In the creation of these devices the designer can take unusual liberties with letterforms, as in the monogram (195) where the initials jk are welded into a single unit, the lowercase j being turned round and the dot completing the top lefthand corner of the design. See also (17), (18), (42), (104), (135), (178) and the monogram on page 11.

The logotype (196) has an unusual form of T – a combination of capital and lowercase forms – which adds considerably to the unity and flow of the design. In designs of this kind, the limited number of letters forces the designer to try many permutations of form and style in his search for a unique and satisfying unity. A good design will have a feeling of inevitability about it, and will avoid forced or contrived conjunctions of letters. Several illustrations in this book would make a good basis for logotypes, see (23), (64), (108), (121), (138), (156), (168), (172), (173), (175), (176), (179), (181), (183) and (186).

FOR

FOLLO

FUN

FUNCTION

Legibility versus Pattern

Every lettering design is two things at once: it is language made visible and it is an abstract visual pattern. This can be expressed as the legibility-pattern scale. At one end is the public sign which must make no concessions to pattern-making in its rigorous clarity, but which is nevertheless, if it is well designed, a decorative object. At the opposite end is a text on the wall of a church, which is part of the church's architectural fabric and whose abstract patterns express a sense of truth and wonder – as do the great illuminated initial letters in the *Book of Kells* – yet which is also intended to be read.

The designer usually works somewhere between these two extremes, and must decide in each case where on the legibility-pattern scale his work should come. Legibility, therefore, is dependent on function, and function usually insists on legibility. For the most part this book has been concerned with the principles of lettering design which ensure legibility, but at the same time it recognises and encourages the pattern-making potential of this two-sided art. Lettering design must follow the best modern design practice, which is succinctly expressed in the famous dictum of the architect Louis Sullivan, *form follows function*.

M
WS
CTION

GLOSSARY OF LETTERING TERMS

AMPERSAND, the combination of *et* (Latin for *and*) into a single character, &.

ASCENDER, stroke of any lowercase (*q.v.*) letter which extends above the x-height (*q.v.*), b,d, etc.

BLACKLETTER, a heavy and angular medieval letterform. See (75), (90), (187) and (192).

BOWL, the curved part of certain letters, d,p, etc.

BRACKET, the rounded junction of a serif (*q.v.*) with a stroke. Variation in its shape affects the character of the letter.

CALLIGRAPHY, formal hand-writing.

CAPITALS, the majuscule alphabet derived from Roman inscriptions. Also called uppercase in printing.

CLARENDON, a letter style with bold bracketted (*q.v.*) serifs (*q.v.*), also known as Ionic, 19th century. See (79).

CONTRAST, the variation between thick and thin letter-strokes. See page 109.

COPPERPLATE, an engraved letter style developed from italic script but with a greater slope, 18th century. See (99).

COUNTER, the space enclosed or partly enclosed by a letter.

DESCENDER, stroke of any lowercase (*q.v.*) letter which extends below the x-height (*q.v.*), g,j, etc.

EGYPTIAN, a letter style similar to Clarendon (*q.v.*) without brackets to the serifs (*q.v.*), 19th century.

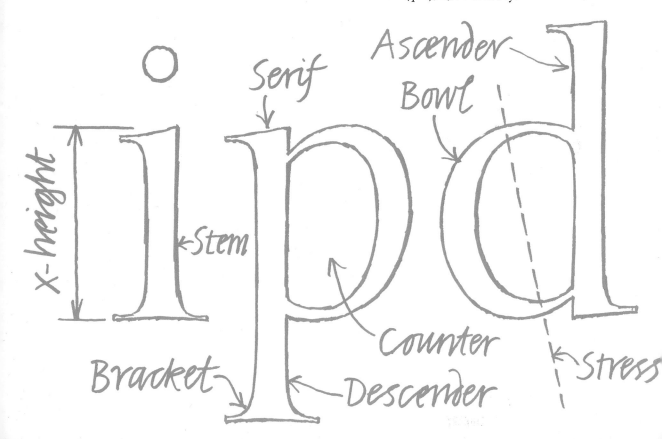

FATFACE, a letter style with a very strong contrast (*q.v.*), 19th century. See (79).

FLOURISH, the extension of a letter-stroke into a graceful curve. See page 117.

GROTESQUE (GROT), another name for sans serif (*q.v.*) letters, 19th century.

HAIRLINE, the thinnest part of a letter.

HALF UNCIAL, pen letter similar to uncial (*q.v.*) with more ascenders (*q.v.*) and descenders (*q.v.*), from 5th to 9th centuries. See (88).

ITALIC, a sloped letter style based on 16th century Chancery script.

LOGOTYPE, a design in which letter style and word(s) do not change, as in a trademark or masthead (*q.v.*). See page 155.

LOWERCASE, the small letter alphabet based on minuscules (*q.v.*), not capitals. Printing term.

MASTHEAD, the name at the head of a newspaper, magazine, etc.

MINUSCULE, pen letter developed from half uncial (*q.v.*), from 9th to 13th centuries. Promoted by Charlemagne (Carolignian minuscule) and later used as a model for early roman lowercase (*q.v.*) type. See (89).

MODERN FACE, letters with a strong contrast (*q.v.*) and vertical stress (*q.v.*). See (111).

MONOGRAM, a combination of initial letters into a single design. See page 155.

OLD FACE, letters with oblique stress (*q.v.*). 16th to 18th century typefaces and later designs based on this style. See (93).

ROMAN, capital (*q.v.*) and lowercase (*q.v.*) letters with thick and thin strokes and serifs (*q.v.*).

RUSTIC CAPITALS, a condensed written version of roman capitals, with thin vertical strokes and thick horizontal strokes, up to 6th century. See (86).

SANS SERIF, letters without serifs (*q.v.*) and usually having strokes of apparently even thickness. Also called Grotesque.

SERIF, the finishing stroke at the end of a stem (*q.v.*) or other letter-stroke.

STEM, the vertical stroke of a letter.

STRESS, the angle of the thickest part of a bowl (*q.v.*).

SWASH LETTERS, flourished letters used as alternatives to normal characters in italic (*q.v.*) alphabets.

TUSCAN, a letter style with bifurcated serifs (*q.v.*), common in 19th century but also used earlier. See (80) and (126).

TYPE, letters cast in metal, or exposed on film, which are used in combination for printing.

UNCIAL, pen letter capitals (*q.v.*) in which round characters replace some of the usual forms, from 5th to 9th centuries. See (87). Originally uncial meant 'inch high'.

UPPERCASE, the printing term for capitals (*q.v.*).

X-HEIGHT, the height of lowercase (*q.v.*) letters without ascenders (*q.v.*) or descenders (*q.v.*).

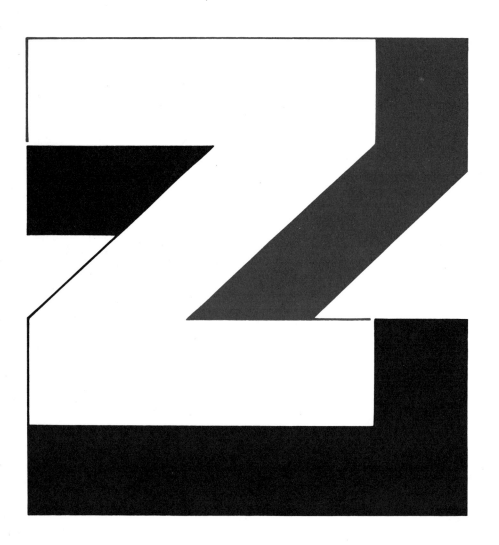